The Muse Is In:

An Owner's Manual to Your Creativity

By
Jill Badonsky

RUNNING PRESS
PHILADELPHIA · LONDON

Books published by Running Press are available at special discounts for bulk purchases in the United States by corporations, institutions, and other organizations. For more information, please contact the Special Markets Department at the Perseus Books Group, 2300 Chestnut Street, Suite 200, Philadelphia, PA 19103, or call (800) 810-4145, ext. 5000, or e-mail special.markets@perseusbooks.com.

ISBN 978-0-7624-4467-0
Library of Congress Control Number: 2012939379
E-book ISBN 978-0-7624-4710-7

9   8   7   6   5   4   3   2   1
Digit on the right indicates the number of this printing

Cover and interior design by Jill Badonsky
Edited by Jennifer Kasius

Running Press Book Publishers
2300 Chestnut Street
Philadelphia, PA 19103-4371

Visit us on the web! www.runningpress.com
Visit www.themuseisin.com for other selections from Jill Badonsky.

You will see this fish throughout the Manual. ➤
He's there as a reminder of your passion for creativity.
When you see him, know that you can choose to swim deep
or stay shallow with your creativity.
Take a deep breath into the vastness of your being; follow its flow.
See page 33 for a relevant quote from David Lynch's quote.

TABLE OF CONTENTS

"The object isn't to make art, it's to be in that wonderful state which makes art inevitable."
~Robert Henri

MORE CONTENTS

GIZMOS TO POWER UP YOUR CREATIVITY

You will recognize your own path when you come upon it because suddenly you will have all the energy and imagination you need. ~Jerry Gillies

CREATIVITY THINKING TOOLS

TROUBLESHOOTING:

DAY-TO-DAY MAINTENANCE DATEBOOK

ENDING STUFF

PREFACE

creativity

I LOVE CREATIVITY SO
I WROTE THIS MANUAL.
~JILL BADONSKY

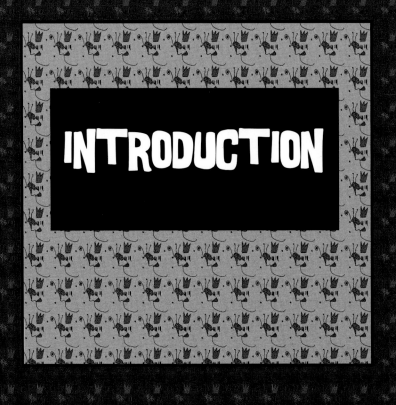

INTRODUCTION

INCLUDES:

Hi Creativity Owner,

You own a dazzling feature of the human experience called CREATIVITY. Despite rumors to the contrary, everyone has it. So . . . are you using yours? If you don't know how, you're in the right place. If you DO know how . . . you're in the right place too–creativity just keeps taking you deeper if you operate it often.

This here Owner's Manual will help you to use your creativity to its fullest potential so you don't miss out on any of its spellbinding features (of which there is a collossal amount.) It will also help you troubleshoot annoying blocks that tend to disrupt smooth creating and cause crankiness.

Owner's Manuals can be perplexing, this one--not so much. Making it easy to show up for your creativity is one of the things that WORKS so begin using that tool right away by asking this question frequently: "How can I make this easier?" There is no need to make things harder, but people frequently do. **Keep this manual handy at all times (within reason), for ideas all about "easier."**

Since we will be embarking upon this journey together, let's make sure we know where to meet in case we get separated. I'm thinking at the cupcake stand . . . is that okay with you? We won't always be doing things simultaneously, especially because you tend to skip around a lot. But no worries, feel free to bounce around in the manual as much as you like because creativity IS non-linear.

Open the manual to any page and on that page will probably be a message you could use; if you can't figure it out, just make it up because that counts as being creative too. And don't forget to breathe.

Breathing is a lot like creativity: As you inhale, you receive an inspiration, you let it run through the unique magnificence of who you are, and then you release it into the world, letting it go, unattached to the way it needs to look. An exhale.

I bet you just took a breath right then, didn't you? You're so impressionable. Most creative people are. We're malleable.

Of course, in the creative process you will be adding words, paint strokes, dance steps, guitar strums, garden gnomes, or your unique twist to your exhale, but the process will be invigorating especially if your passages are clear. To clear stuffy passages, send your inner critic out for a cappuccino and then move to another state. If you can't do that, you can use the less complicated solutions provided in this manual. There's a plethora of them.

The next step to activating your creativity is to simply believe you CAN be creative, even if it's just a tiny more belief than you had a minute ago. If you already have "belief," get ready, because creativity has no limits; the more you use your creativity, the more the world will continue to unfold with gentle, illustrious wonder. Trust me.

When your creativity runs on Muse control, you may discover you're a playwright, a sculptor, a kitchen-table comedian, a beacon of creative kindness, or a person who chooses grace over ego and

contentment over greed. And in that choice you will create a world of joy within yourself; you'll be an artist of *living life*.

With proper care and maintenance, your creativity will be fully operational for the rest of your life. So just take the next little step–the smaller you make it, the more likely you'll take it.

Like . . . just turn the page.

Start your engines,

The Muse is IN

CUPcakes

THE POSSIBLE PATH OF AN IDEA
(Idea paths may vary)

1. YOU FALL IN LOVE WITH AN IDEA.
Systems Check:
Physiological - Exhilaration
Spiritual - Electricity
Mental - Optimism (both delusional and real), Rapid Fire Thinking
Emotional - A lot like Infatuation

Action Recommended: SAY YES!

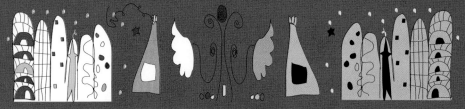

Between the idea and the reality . . . falls the Shadow ~T.S. Eliot

2. THE USUAL DEMONS SHOW UP (They're just part of the process.)

Creative Chaos:	What the . . . ?
Resistance:	You can't make me!
Fear:	Pick your flavor, many to choose from.
Perfectionism:	It never seems to be good enough.
Overwhelm:	There's . . . just . . . too . . . much!
Procrastination:	(Not available for comment, over on Facebook, etc.)
No Time:	Maybe I should shoot the TV!
Ruthless Self-Talk:	I'm SO not worthy.
Self Sabotage:	I messed up.. and I think I did it on purpose.

Systems Check:
Physiological - Immoblized, or at best twitchy.
Spiritual - Out to Lunch
Mental - Stuck or Distracted
Emotional - Frustrated, Embarrassed, Cranky

Action Recommended: TROUBLESHOOT!

(See Troubleshooting on Page 83. Flip there now before you end up putting this under your bed with all your other Self-Help books.)

3. DO IT ANYWAY

Follow the directions in the next chapters to: Get in the
right state of mind with willingness, courage, patience,
focus, passion, and comfort with solitude.

Use the Manual's Gizmos that make creativity easier:
reminders, small steps, low expectations, time tricks,
self-talk that works, a break, meditation,
kid-like thinking and others. See page 39.

Action Recommended:
FULL SPEED AHEAD
WITH PATIENCE
REPEAT AS NEEDED

Systems Check:
All systems poised for overcoming obstacles.

4. TAKE YOUR IDEAS TO NEW HEIGHTS

Your good ideas can be tweaked into even better ones with the Creativity Tools
you'll find in the Manual. Some ideas are meant to start out bad. Just keep going.

    * Mind-map, list, free associate
    * Associate
    * Modify
    * See your idea many different ways using different attitudes, personas,
      and action words to trigger new perspectives.

See page 63

Live it, breathe it—don't stop at the obvious but stop before the energy of your idea
is gone.
Put it down for awhile and return refreshed.

Systems Check:
All systems having a blast.

Action Recommended:
EXPLORE, HAVE FUN

5. SINK INTO THE PROCESS

~ Get into the beloved timeless flow that takes you to the otherworldly
   places of the mind and the soul.
~ Make it up as you go along or read the directions and then modify them.
~ Believe in yourself or at the very least, act as if you do.
~ Use the Day-to-Day Maintenance Datebook to practice (on page 108).

ink

Systems Check:
When in the flow, all systems—physical,
mental, spiritual, and emotional—are
in their most optimal state.

Action Recommended:
COMPLY WITH THE MAGIC
KEEP PRACTICING

6. STAY!

Persevere and practice. Troubleshoot each new challenge, acknowledge every success,
embrace the intention to make the process fun, let go of rigid expectations.

Systems Check:
Steady, nonlinear, sometimes taking a
break, always returning.

Action Recommended:
KEEP GOING, GIVE IT A CHANCE

7. CELEBRATE AND REPEAT

Systems Check:
Fulfilled

Action Recommended:
MAINTAIN YOUR
CREATIVITY

SNEAKING IN THE BACK DOOR

Sometimes creativity works best if you go in through the back door, which means approaching your process in sneaky and unpredictable ways to avoid having your usual obstacles stop you.

USE NO-BRAINER INSPIRATION:
The relaxed and intuitive state of creativity often shows up in the shower, while driving, doing the dishes, walking, or during other no-brainer activities. Start your creative time in no-brain-land where the left-brain critic is relaxed so right brain inspiration is more easily accessed.

ACT NONCHALANT:
Starting an activity with the intention of just playing to pass the time or have fun can relax the same pressure that turns into creative blocks. Make time for just toying with something, not for the best seller, the perfect art or the brilliant invention.

HAVE A HEART-TO-HEART TALK WITH YOURSELF:
Making time for creativity affects every other part of your life. If you're putting off your creative passion because you think you have more important things to do, think again. You will deplete your joy and effectiveness as mate, employee, parent, and pet owner. Free your soul-energy; do those creative things you love to do, even if their only purpose is to make the rest of your life better.

USE CREATIVE FOREPLAY:
Use the moments in between your other activities to fantasize about your creativity. Ask compelling questions, imagine the feeling of your creative bliss, and recall an especially enjoyable moment. You will notice a marked increase in your desire to go further. Submit to your urges with wild abandon.

HAVE A TRYST WITH YOUR CREATIVITY:
Sneak time with your creativity behind the back of all your other activities. This sneakiness evokes mischievousness, which begets the allure of the clandestine, which gets the attention of the kid-like energy inside of you and tricks it into engaging in the same creativity you were resisting a minute ago. **Reverse Psychology:** Say you are going to do one thing and then do your creative passion instead–this works especially well for the rebellious. Actually list: Clean the garage, restock the cupcake supplies, write bills , etc. THEN, write your poem or paint a picture of the eclipse INSTEAD!!! (snicker).

BE A FREEDOM FIGHTER:
Pretend that you're a creative freedom fighter defending your kingdom of authentic expression. Let the world know how determined, skilled, and powerful you are . . . and you will begin to BE determined, skilled, powerful and CREATIVE. Save the world from the mundane. Wearing a cape can be dangerous, be careful.

THE DUHS

A dose of the obvious to help you operate with eyes open. Lubricate your common sense with these points that calibrate more creativity.

1. Beating yourself up doesn't work as well as being fascinated by who you are and the things you do.

Constant self-deprecation works as well as hammering on a sprouting daisy when it first pops through the soil.

Despite work environments where intimidation and high pressure have resulted in productivity, creativity responds to positive reinforcement, inner-applause, and Hershey's Kisses.

Be compassionate with yourself; creativity is fragile but can express the depth of your soul in bewilderingly brave and brilliant ways.

2. You get more done when you start things than when you don't.

J. R. R. Tolkien once said, "It's a job that's never started that takes the longest to finish," and along the same train of thought, Will Rogers added, "Even if you are on the right track, you'll get run over if you just sit there." To start: Point yourself in the direction of your Creative Adventure and take a step. One step leads to the next, but sometimes just one step in and of itself is better than none.

3. Comparison is Lethal in the Creative Process.

If you compare your efforts on a pursuit you've just begun with the efforts of people who have spent a lot time doing the same kind of thing, it will discourage you. And, WHY would you wanna DO that? Think about it. THINK ABOUT IT.

Okay, back to my indoor voice. Decide to ask yourself how the progress of others can inspire you rather than making yourself miserable and discouraged with comparison. Everyone has their own path and timeline, honor your own and if you're procastinating, check out the Troubleshooting Section on page 83 for help.

13

4. Give Yourself Permission.

Maybe this one isn't so obvious. In a world where you fall prey to unrealistically high expectations, giving yourself permission to relax, play, find time for creativity, and not sabotage yourself can power up your particpation. It's suspiciously wonderful how a simple declaration of permission to be imperfect can be so freeing. Try it.

5. Thinking you will work for long blocks of time at the beginning of the process is a setup for failure.

Now that you've quit your job, cleared your schedule, carved out three hours, you finally have large blocks of time to be creative. Right? Ha, ha, ha, ha, ha, snort, ha.

Those with experience with this phenomenon are laughing too, because when you set aside large blocks of time and are not accustomed to working for that long, there's a good chance large blocks of resistance will show up.

So develop your perseverance muscles by showing up in small increments of time and then you will eventually be able to stay longer and longer. Start with five minutes.

6. Do it Now.

You don't need to take a class, earn a degree, build an art studio, get a desk, go on a retreat, or break up with your boyfriend and move to New York, to begin. Many people delay getting started because they think they need certain conditions. These are avoidance strategies. Each time you achieve one of these make-believe requirements you'll find some new requirement that needs to happen before you begin. Blow them off, sit in your closet without any formal education, and write a book, even if there's a party in the next room.

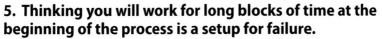

"Do not wait until the conditions are
perfect to begin.
Beginning makes the conditions perfect."
~Alan Cohen

QUIZ:
ARE YOU CREATIVE?

1. Are you breathing?

If you answered "YES" to the above question, you are or can be creative.

If you answered "NO," reincarnate soon, unless you don't believe in that stuff.

"CREATIVITY IS A MINDSET, AN ATTITUDE. REGARDLESS OF HOW WE FEEL—LOW OR HIGH OR IN BETWEEN—CREATIVITY IS ALWAYS THERE."
-NIKKI COULOMBE

You know how some people say, "I am SO not creative," or "I don't have a creative bone in my body"? If you're one of them, here are some explanations as to why you say that:

1. You think creativity is only about making art, music, and writing and don't realize that it's also about choosing an attitude, being a clever boss, mate, parent, friend, or neighbor; it's about coming up with unique solutions, approaches, and responses. It's about how you do everything in your life.

2. You have unrealistic expectations of being creative, comparing yourself to others and feeling inferior when you haven't even begun to do what it takes to get to where those people got.

3. You are afraid someone will ask you to be creative and feel foolish if you fail to meet your own unreasonable expectations.

4. You are not aware of the power of the tools in this Manual. Good thing you own it.

5. You are afraid you won't be perfect and you equate being perfect with being valued as a person.

6. You are afraid, period. It is normal for creativity to bring up a swarm of fears.

7. Someone once said something discouraging about an attempt you made to be creative, you made the mistake of believing them and it felt really bad.

8. You tried for five or ten minutes to be creative and it didn't take. You are unaware that creativity requires persevered practice.

9. You have created a belief that works against the belief that you are creative.

"The human mind, after all, has the creative impulse built into its operating system, hardwired into its most esstential programming code." ~Jonah Lehrer

 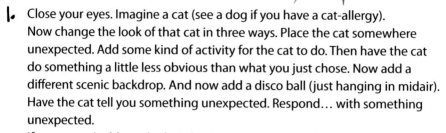

EASY EXERCISES

1. Close your eyes. Imagine a cat (see a dog if you have a cat-allergy). Now change the look of that cat in three ways. Place the cat somewhere unexpected. Add some kind of activity for the cat to do. Then have the cat do something a little less obvious than what you just chose. Now add a different scenic backdrop. And now add a disco ball (just hanging in midair). Have the cat tell you something unexpected. Respond… with something unexpected.

If you weren't able to do that short exercise, you are simply resistant or unwilling. Resistance is a creative block; it does not mean you are not creative. If you *were* able to do the cat exercise, you are creative. The more you practice little exercises like this, the more creative you will become in the way that YOU are creative, which is different from the way of anyone else.

2. Take a deep breath. As you exhale relax your shoulders. You just *created* relaxation.

3. Listen to all the voices that judge, worry, belittle, and protect you. Now imagine those voices are not you. You are the self inside of you to whom they are talking. Imagine that self as a pure kid-like, creative soul ready to combine, associate, invent, modify, shift, amuse, or make sculptures out of magic. You just *created* peace, amusement, or maybe delight and eagerness. These things lead to enjoyment and enjoying the process is one of the keys to perseverance.

Put all the voices that don't work for you on a bus to summer camp (even if it's winter) and wave good-bye. The canoe rides will mellow them out.

EVERYONE GETS TO BE CREATIVE

The creativity you played with in the Easy Exercises is from the same mechanism responsible for generating ideas in art, writing, and music. It's just that those avenues require some instruction, practice, perseverance, self-esteem, focus, dedicated small steps, and willingness to be an awkward beginner over and over.

Those are the creative Gizmos we talk about in this manual. They make creativity easier. If you don't have them, you can get them. Read on.

Some people think we are either born with creativity or we're not. Many people are indeed born with an innate talent. When they cultivate that talent through many, many hours of practice, amazing works of art, literature, music, what-have-you are brought into existence. But really, do you need to BE that person in order to discover the bliss, benefits, and rewards of creativity? No.

You can develop skill with practice, but the process is what makes life more wonderful. Talented people are not necessarily happy; the ones who are also happy, know how to *create* joy within themselves.

Passion, curiosity, healing, need, problem-solving, angst, joy, amusement, reckless abandon, these are ALSO drives that result in creativity. Everyone has the ability to be creative in these ways.
Everyone gets to be creative.

CREATIVITY'S FRINGE BENEFITS

MUSE TRANSLATION:

The rewards you receive from the creative process far exceed that which you set out to attain, but only if you relax your expectations, pay attention, and adjust your settings more for discovery rather than control.

ENGAGING IN THE CREATIVE PROCESS AND PERSEVERING DESPITE THE DIFFICULTIES IT CAN GIVE YOU:

✪ Self-respect

Versatile problem-solving abilities and coping skills:

- ▣ Skills of acceptance
- ▣ resourcefulness
- ▣ perspective
- ▣ flexibility
- ▣ resilience
- ▣ patience
- ▣ grace
- ▣ tolerance
- ▣ humor

✪ THE FEELING OF BEING CREATIVE IS SYNONYMOUS WITH JOY AND FULFILLMENT.

✪ Enhanced ingenuity, distinction, and influence
✪ A surge of liberating individualism as you define your authentic voice
✪ A confidence that can move you forward in every other aspect of your life because you are more willing to take risks, try new things, and believe in yourself

The arts are not a way of making a living. They are a very human way of making life more bearable.
~Kurt Vonnegut

19

IN THE CREATIVE PROCESS, YOU ALSO GAIN:

- A new repertoire of interests to lift you out of life's drudgery
- The freedom and power that come with flexibility of thought
- The peak experience of engaging in the process of creation
- The deep reward of sharing talents and connecting with the human condition
- A higher capacity and more avenues for delight
- Awareness, attention, better focus, and concentration on the pleasures of life
- Healthy and rewarding outlets to sublimate challenging emotions
- Optimum healing: physically, emotionally, and spiritually
- Less preoccupation with worrying about what others think
- A world where you can invent, control, manipulate, change, destroy, guide, and construct without getting arrested
- Depth of character: You become more interesting and attractive inside and out; creative people have natural and effortless magnetism
- More autonomy and more control over your life and, ultimately, more reason to live

NO MATTER WHAT THE TANGIBLE OUTCOME IS, YOU CANNOT HELP BUT
BECOME A BETTER PERSON WHEN YOU FOLLOW A CREATIVE CALL.
IF YOU FOCUS ON THE PRODUCT, YOU GET FLEETING SATISFACTION FROM
AN END RESULT.
IF YOU FOCUS ON THE PROCESS YOU GET A LIFE,
BECAUSE LIFE IS A PROCESS.

CREATIVITY STARTERS

READ THIS LIST OF REAL AND ABSTRACT AGENTS OF CREATIVE INSPIRATION TO SHIFT THE GEARS OF YOUR MIND FROM LOGIC TO IMAGINATIVE, POETIC POSSIBILITY.

PAINTS
A PIANO, TROMBONE, KAZOO, FIDDLE, FLUTE, GUITAR, VIOLIN
PAPER, PEN, PENCIL
WAX PAPER
ANGST
TWO UNRELATED CONCEPTS
A LOOSE ASSOCIATION
A DANCE STEP
FREE-FLOATING ANXIETY
THE FEELING OF GRACE
BALLOONS
CANVAS
LONELINESS
CELEBRATION
ALTRUISM
INFATUATION
HEARTBREAK

AN IMAGINARY FRIEND
A FAVORITE LYRIC
A THOUGHT THAT TAKES YOUR BREATH AWAY
AN ECHO
A SMILE
A ROAD TRIP
A CAMERA
A CACTUS
THE BREEZE
BROKEN DISHES
A LOST PRAYER
FOUND OBJECTS
A REUNION
A SCREECH
THAT THING YOUR KID SAYS
THE ANSWER, "YES"
A TRAIN TRIP

GARDENING TOOLS
A PAPER CLIP
A RANDOM THOUGHT
A SHOWER
AN MP3 PLAYER
TWIGS AND WIRE
A STOVE
THE SKY
FOOTPRINTS
DUCT TAPE
A THIN BLACK MICRON PEN
TEARS
THE NEGATIVE SPACE
PINS, NEEDLES, THREAD
SCRAPS
AN ARGUMENT
AN AGREEMENT
CAPTURED EAVESDROPS
A MISTAKE
A MEMORY
A MISHEARD LYRIC
A STRANGER'S ACCENT
THE ANGLE OF LIGHT

A LAUGH
A LOOK FROM A DOG
BARE FEET
A PAUSE
A SIDEWAYS GLANCE
COOKIE DOUGH
AN OBSESSION
DAWN
A DOODLE
WORDLESSNESS
FREEDOM
ENDINGS

CREATIVE EXPRESSION STARTERS

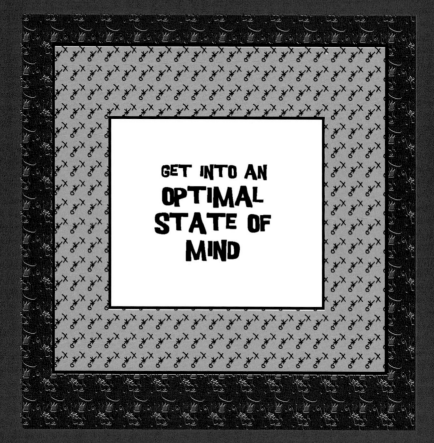

GET INTO AN
OPTIMAL
STATE OF
MIND

FINE-TUNING TOOLS:

MIND IN "READY" MODE

COURAGE

PATIENCE

FOCUS

PASSION

SOLITUDE

WILLINGNESS

MIND IN "READY" MODE

Get familiar with the parts of the mind needed for creativity to function optimally.

If anything is missing, don't be alarmed. Act naturally. Pretend you're writing something in your notebook. People will think you're being creative.

You are.

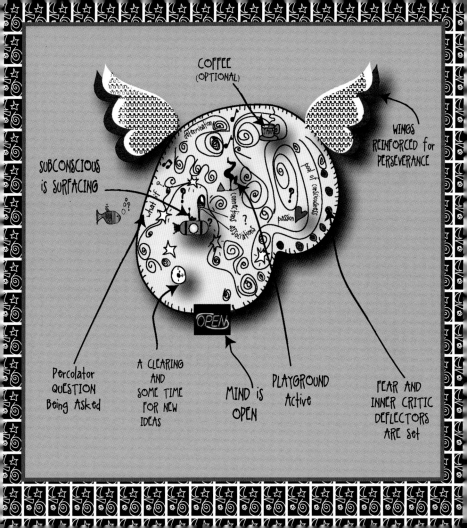

courage

EVERYONE HAS TALENT. WHAT IS RARE IS THE COURAGE TO FOLLOW THE TALENT TO THE DARK PLACE WHERE IT LEADS.
~ERICA JONG

LIFE SHRINKS OR EXPANDS IN PROPORTION TO ONE'S COURAGE. ~ANAIS NIN

IF EVERYONE LIKES WHAT I'VE DONE, I HAVEN'T GONE FAR ENOUGH TO STAY TRUE TO MYSELF.
~THE MUSE

Showing the world something you've made is like saying, "Look, I created something that is completely new and untested, birthed from the fragile center of my very being, and now I'm subjecting it to the judgment of the cold cruel world?"

Creating something is an act of courage.

Courage doesn't mean having no fear; it means staying with your creative journey despite all the fears that come up. Courage is remaining true to your creative call despite doubts, the risk of rejection, giving up security, and experiencing setbacks and failure.

To be courageous is exhilarating; it corrals all the butterflies of anxiety that flutter in your belly and uses their energy for forward movement.

I'VE BEEN ABSOLUTELY TERRIFIED EVERY MOMENT OF MY LIFE - AND I'VE NEVER LET IT KEEP ME FROM DOING A SINGLE THING I WANTED TO DO. ~GEORGIA O'KEEFFE

Courage removes the hesitancy to try out new ideas, fuels innovation, and is required in order to live a deeply creative life. If you're not 100% courageous, you can develop courage gradually by taking one tiny step after another and embracing the reward of confidence.

PUSH THIS BUTTON TO ACTIVATE YOUR COURAGE 5% MORE. THEN ASK, "WHAT WILL I DO WITH A LITTLE MORE COURAGE TODAY?"

This page intentionally left blank so as not to detract from the importance of the page over there. ⟶

PATIENCE

YOU NEED a **LOT** of
PATIENCE to do CREATIVE things.

Things take time. Sometimes years. Don't give up.
Take a break, breathe, be Kind,
and give yourself a chance.
Trust is a good accessory to add to Patience.

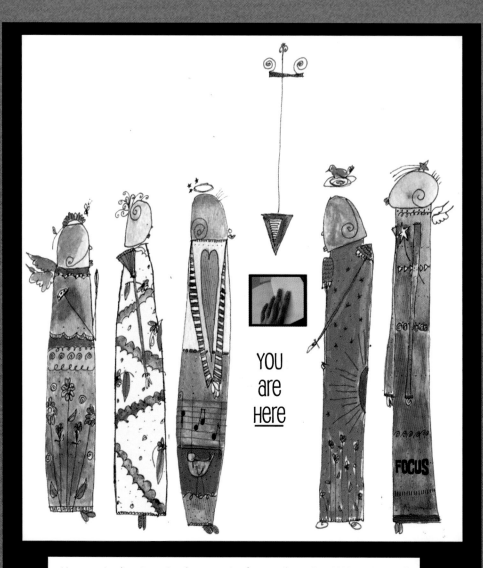

YOU
are
HERE

You can't plug into A when you're focused on B, r, X,Y, a piece of drifting fuzz, what's for lunch, who liked your Facebook post, and the buzz coming from the light fixture in the kitchen. You need to STAY here . . . and focus.

ADJUST YOUR LENS FOR A CLOSE-UP
OF ONE THING AT A TIME

Focusing is one of the biggest challenges Creative Adventurers face these days.
Your attention span may have gotten into the habit of rapidly hitchhiking from
one flashing image to another, resulting in a supershort attention span.
What you may not realize is how captive you are to this habit that keeps you from
paying attention where it truly counts.

ADJUST YOUR FOCUS WITH THESE QUESTIONS:

What does it feel like to be singularly focused?
When's the last time you felt that?
What was the quality of those moments?
What did you love about being so focused?
Are you willing to move from the hypnosis of multi-tasking
to the genius of a focused mind?
Were you able to focus on theses questions?

Are you willing to step away from the iPhone, the iPod, the iPad, the i-Can-Only-
Guess-What-Else with undivided attention for your Creative Adventure?
Are you willing to establish creative focus as your new habit?
If you answered "yes," start with small steps.

YOU HAVE PERMISSION TO BE PRESENT.
TAKE NOTES: WRITING DOWN YOUR IDEAS, THOUGHTS,
AND INSPIRATIONS IMPROVES YOUR FOCUS.
BE WILLING TO STEP AWAY FROM THE DISTRACTIONS.

PASSION

CREATIVITY IS MY   OXYGEN

Ideas are like fish. If you want to catch little fish, you can stay in the shallow water. But if you want to catch the big fish, you've got to go deeper. ~David Lynch

PASSION TAKES YOU DEEP

The willful determination that has been the ticket to success for countless creative greats is made of passion—it's an unstoppable energy fueled by intense desire, resulting in the making of miracles.

UNLOCK THE POWER OF YOUR PASSION BY:

1. Celebrating your individuality with fiery determination. Express your unique singularity and experience deep fulfillment.

2. Embracing mortality. You're not here forever, let go of complacency and denial, stop delaying, take those risks, and begin with tiny steps. Summon up the strength to let go of those pastimes that are not moving you where you want to go, or at least ration out your time gradually to more creative pursuits.

3. Loving yourself enough to change your experience of being alive by cultivating your version of creativity.

4. Running away without leaving home: Create new worlds, explore, process, sublimate, transcend the dark side of life, meet up with another dimension, and establish yourself as a beacon of inspiration. Creativity does all this without any other resource than your mind. But none of it will happen without your ardent devotion.

ACTIVATION QUESTIONS:

What would it feel like to really be passionate about my Creative Adventure?

If you don't know what your passion is, use Percolator Questions:
What's one small way I can discover my passion?
What excited me with delight when I was a child?
What are others doing that creates a sense of heightened energy in me when I hear about it?
Was I ever passionate? If yes, what was I doing?
What am I willing to explore in order to find my passion?

SOLITUDE

The writer's first duty is acceptance of solitude. Anything else is not truth. It is in solitude that writers will have their most creative inspirations, see the plots and characters of their stories and novels take shape, and produce their most important work.
~Henry Miller

ACTIVATION OF SOLITUDE:

Ask: Do I have enough time to myself?
If the answer is **NO**:
Imagine a time when you can be alone with your Muse.
Imagine the feeling of inspired solitude; feel it right now, in this moment.
Team up passion, determination, and focus to make solitude possible.

Daydreaming is a valid part of the creative process. Don't let anyone tell you otherwise. In our society, many believe that tangible productivity is the only thing that counts.

In the creative process, daydreaming makes connections and discoveries possible.

Daydreaming happens best in solitude, as does depth of thought, ephiphanies, reception of new ideas, and awakening to possibilities–both the obvious and the mysterious ones.

WITHOUT GREAT SOLITUDE
NO SERIOUS WORK IS POSSIBLE.
~CARL SANDBURG

Willingness

YES!

Willingness can be as easy as a slight shift from less time spent on the Internet (or with TV) to five minutes more in creative wonder.

If your Willingness is flimsy because you haven't used it for a while, add patient determination and take a really small step. Any step will do. The smaller it is, the more you will be . . . willing.

Go through the list of things that successful Creative Adventurers are willing to do. (It's over on your right.) Add up the number of boxes you check, divide by five apples, eat three oranges, floss, determine how fast your train of thought is moving, and then ask yourself this:
How can I make my Creative Adventure fun?
Notice your willingness multiply.

Doing everything on the list at once is not required or even advised. Unrealistic expectations and ruthless pressure cause Willingness to backfire into discouragement, feeling overwhelmed, and resistance. Avoid loading too much on your circuits. Be light.

Are you Willing to:

1. Focus:

- [ ] Let go of distractions? (Even if it's just a few moments less than last time?)
- [ ] Stop putting off those things that are most important to your soul and spirit?
- [ ] Love yourself more, feel more deserving, and stop punishing yourself by procrastinating?

2. Spend time alone:

- [ ] Practicing and participating in trial and error, error, error, trial, and "AHA!"
- [ ] Daydreaming?
- [ ] Revising, veering, rethinking, searching?
- [ ] Exposing yourself to stimulating ideas?
- [ ] Entering the spheres that require the deep thought and concentration that takes your idea deeper into a frontier not possible with constant outer stimulation?

3. Persevere:

- [ ] After the enthusiasm of the idea goes away?
- [ ] Through creative chaos, ambiguity, doubt, and frustrations?
- [ ] Through what seems impossible and through uncontrollable delays?
- [ ] Through failure and mixed reviews?
- [ ] Even after an emergency, a break-up, heartburn, something spectacular, a long break, or something unexpected interrupts your rhythm?

4. Replace Voices from the Inner Critic With:

- [ ] Voices that make perseverance possible, of belief and encouragement?
- [ ] The fuel from compliments given by others?
- [ ] Common sense?

5. Be Clever and Free to:

- [ ] Imbue your effort with the magic of who you are?
- [ ] Let go of what others think even if it's just a little at a time?
- [ ] Test drive "bold" and "audacious" and even sometimes, "cocky"?
- [ ] Forge into new territories emotionally, artistically, maybe even physically?

6. Go Past the Obvious to the Not So Obvious:

- [ ] Not always stopping with the first right answer and searching for more answers?
- [ ] But not dismissing your first response if it really feels like it's the best?

7. Detach from:

- [ ] Rigid expectations as to how things need to look, sound or end up?
- [ ] Something you think is brilliant but really needs to be worked on or eliminated?
- [ ] Your ego?
- [ ] Things going exactly the way you want them to go?
- [ ] The way things were done in the past and the supposed, "right way"?
- [ ] The need to be perfect or best?

NINE GIZMOS
TO POWER-UP
YOUR
CREATIVITY

1. REALLY SMALL STEPS
2. LOWERED EXPECTATIONS
3. MAKING TIME
4. SELF-KINDNESS
5. PROCESS FUEL
6. TAKING A BREAK
7. MEDITATION
8. BE A KID
9. REMINDERS

REALLY SMALL STEPS

NICKNAME: This really works.

DESCRIPTION:

Break down projects, intentions, desired thoughts and feelings into really, REALLY small action steps and increments of time. This will make starting your creative engine easier, kinder, and more enticing. The irony is that small steps will actually get you further than trying to take big steps that result in procrastination, resistance, or becoming overwhelmed.

If you have to get a lot done quickly, set your intention for 15 minutes, take a break, resume, and repeat. Notice what happens.

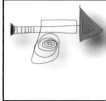

INDICATIONS FOR USE:

Use when you want to start something, return to something, feel a more empowering feeling, change a pattern, do something that seems hard to get started, or just enjoy the gentle brilliance of small steps.

SUGGESTED QUESTIONS:

How can I break this down smaller? Is that small enough?
What if I broke it down smaller than THAT?
How can I make this project gentler and simpler?
How many things in my life can I apply that question to?

RECOMMENDATIONS

Think of the next small step you'd like to take on your Creative Adventure. If it doesn't seem so ridiculously small that it's almost like you can't not do it, it's too big. (The double negative was intended for effect, so don't not like me because I didn't not do that.) Here are some translations of typical steps made smaller to get people started:

1. Writing: Instead of saying . . . "I need to write for an hour everyday," how about: "I get to turn and face the desk, then take two steps. Then maybe I'll dream about a sentence or two. If I make it to the desk, I'll begin writing with lowered expectations for 5 minutes."

2. Art: Instead of saying . . . "I will spend all day Saturday painting in my studio," how about: "I get to remember the feeling I get when two colors are spread over the paper and just the right texture is created."

You may ask, "How the hell does she get anything done?" Here's what happens:

1. Writing: I ALWAYS make it to the desk and for my next small step: 5 minutes of writing. (But each time it ends up being more. If it was just 5 minutes, I've succeeded and am more likely to return because the energy of succeeding is more magnetic than the energy of missing the mark.)

2 . Art: Just thinking about my process gets me excited about my next step and I am often found in my studio conspiring the collaboration of colors. I lose track of time and three days later come out for a pizza. Small steps make it easier to get started.

SMALL STEP EXAMPLES

• Simply think of one tiny step you can take.

• Pull out a project you haven't worked on for a while, set a timer for 5 minutes, and make it a challenge to do ANYTHING, no matter how small or insignificant. Quality is optional. This is just to get you started.

• Allow yourself to feel 5% more devoted to starting your task, you don't even have to start it, just practice the feeling.

• Take 2 minutes to prepare your space for your next action either the night before: Write an unfinished sentence, set up your notes, arrange your tools, or set a candle and some matches in your space, ready to light to create an atmosphere of inspiration.

• For just 15 seconds feel a full body sensation of the feeling of trust instead of fear, repeat frequently.

• Just open your blog, your program, your notebook . . . and take a little look around.

LOWERED EXPECTATIONS

NICKNAME: [sigh of relief]

DESCRIPTION:

Lowering your expectations will work wonders in getting you started on your creative passion in a gentle, freeing, and unpressured way.

You can't get better if you don't do anything and many people don't do anything when high expectations trigger fear, hesitancy, avoidance, and resistance.

Experiment with approaching your work "purposely bad."

INDICATIONS FOR USE:

Use when you are avoiding your work, when it feels like a huge weight descends on you when you want to get started, when you're not having fun, when you begin again after you've been gone for a while, and when you have a stiff neck and are cranky.

APPLICABLE QUOTATIONS:

"Perfection is spelled PARALYSIS." ~Winston Churchill

"He who hesitates because he feels inferior is being surpassed by he who is busy making mistakes and becoming superior." ~Henry Link

"The reason we struggle with insecurity is because we compare our behind-the-scenes with everyone else's highlight reel." ~Steven Furtick

43

Lowering expectations moves you into the amazing, authentic work your creative engine is capable of because you are doing it with calm authenticity, not oppressed torment.

Pressure may work in cases of advanced creative output where your job is dependent on meeting a deadline and you are used to working under pressure. But if you relax at the beginning of a delicate, divine encounter, hidden genius will not be intimidated from surfacing.

RECOMMENDED SELF-TALK:

• I'm going to approach this like a little kid who doesn't care what it looks like at the beginning.
• I'm lowering my expectations to 60% (rather than the usual 200%).
• I'm just going to relax and let the beginning of this work be whatever it wants without regard to standards, judgment, or it being a measure of my worth as a creative person.

SUGGESTED QUESTIONS:

Where in my creative work can I lower my expectations?

How can I remember that lowering my expectations at the beginning of a process helps me get started and makes it possible for me to improve and excel? Motivational experts mean well and help millions (at least for a little bit). But here's the thing: They usually don't share their own long-and-winding, nonlinear, inconsistent journey to get where they sometimes are, but they expect you to be cured, fixed, or changed completely in 1 week or 30 days. The self-help advice in many books and magazines is unrealistic.

People generally are motivated by new tools for a short amount of time, and because it's too unrealistic to sustain change without long-term practice, they abandon their new direction because their expectations aren't immediately being met in full. They are back at the beginning with a failed experience.

Go for "close enough," and if you can't be consistent, keep showing up when you can. These are humanly doable intentions and get the job done. Let go of the need to be perfect. Do whatever it takes to make showing up comfortable and fun, and then notice how you keep coming back instead of avoiding, procrastinating, or rationalizing why you are doing something else.

44

MAKING TIME

NICKNAME: Show-up

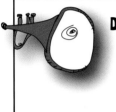

DESCRIPTION:

There IS time to be creative. You sometimes just have to be creative about making it and when you do, be ruthless about protecting it. You may also need to sneak in through the back door to actually USE your time constructively once you've found it because resistance shows up at the front.

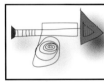

INDICATIONS:

When you need to make time for your Creative Adventure. Make showing up at approximately the same time a habit, then it will feel weird when you don't show up. This is a good weirdness.

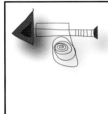

CONTRAINDICATIONS:

1). Saying "I don't have time," is often used as an avoidance strategy for not getting to your creativity. It can be easier to say that than to begin a daunting adventure. 2) Frequently asking yourself, "Why is there never enough time?" will result in creating the reality of never having enough time.

SUGGESTED QUESTIONS:

Where are small moments of time that you can use for your Creative Adventure? When can you simply THINK about the creative process? How can you find more time? (Just keep asking and soon answers will come OR you will just start finding time automatically because the subconscious is being programmed to solve the problem.)
How can I make it easier to use the time when it shows up?

SUMMON UP YOUR ANIMUS

The word animus means "masculine side." In the interest of **time**, I invite you to think of animus in terms of "and-I-must" make time for my creativity because no one else is going to flippin' do it for me." In fact, in most cases people will routinely steal your time. Deciding to tap into animus (installed for selected purposes in both men *and* women), can draw on your forces of ambition, confidence, and tenacity–all important traits in claiming creative time for yourself and not feeling apologetic about it.

Some of you may better relate to this advice: GET SOME BALLS. Tennis balls would work. Write affirmations on them like, "I will be short shot-ing my time with non-creative actions. Love-30." Leave them outside your door. Beach balls are soft enough to throw at people who open the door even when you've asked nicely for some time alone.

But mostly, YOU NEED BALLS, the "and-I-must" be brave kind. Be inspired by artists who DO protect their time. Say with animus, "If they can do it, so can I." (Try that again with more balls.) You taking time for yourself teaches others that making time for creativity is important and ESSENTIAL if you want to be an artist. Clarissa Estes Pinkola's mentions *In Women Who Run With the Wolves*, an artist who does have balls. This sign hangs on her door: "I am working today and am not receiving visitors. I know you think this doesn't mean you because you are my banker, agent, or best friend. But it does." Hang signs if that works for you.

OTHER IDEAS:

~Think Short:
15-30 seconds of creative thought can inspire you, create connections, and activate subconscious processing. 15 seconds is more than most people spend because they believe they have to have big chunks of time in order to do anything. Thinking of your creativity in the time between activities IS being creative.

~Parallel Universe Time:
Team up and work with another person. You don't need to be in the same space, just call before and after.

~Trade Screen-Things for Seen-Things:
Go cold turkey with TV and computer obsessions and you will find an enormous amount of time. Because TV is a tradition for many people they don't count it as a time-suck. It IS totally. Ease yourself away if you need to, or use TV and Internet as rewards AFTER you've spent time with creativity, but if you want to be a creative person, get real. Creativity results in fulfillment. Screen-things? Not so much. Temporary at best. There CAN be a balance if you know your boundaries (and have balls).

HIGH-POWERED SELF-TALK

NICKNAME: Creative power

DESCRIPTION:

• Replacing harsh self-talk with compassion, acceptance, encouragement, and kindness works infinitely better in the creative process.

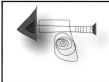

INDICATIONS FOR USE:

When you want to experience the power possible when you think things that indicate that you are on your own side and shift old thought patterns to ones that inspire reved-up action.

CONTRAINDICATIONS:

If you catch yourself beating yourself up, don't beat yourself for beating yourself up. Just give more energy to your compassionate side.

SUGGESTED QUESTIONS:

What can I say to myself that powers up my creative work?
What would it be like to gently catch myself when I'm not kind?
What would it feel like to be on my *own* side for a change?
When have I been kind to myself in the past?
What's something I could say in this minute that would inspire action instead of resistance?
Did I answer the last question or did I simply read it?

EXPLANATION

Suffice it to say that being kind to yourself doesn't always come naturally. Many of us think we need to push and pressure ourselves in order to reach goals, and we ruthlessly call ourselves names without regard to what this is doing to that little spirit inside of us that's in charge of much of our creativity.

Shifting from a lifetime pattern of ruthless self-talk to the kind of gentle talk that kind spirits deliver doesn't happen overnight, so begin practicing now and keep practicing, and then begin again if you forget. Don't expect perfection. If you are realistic and know that it's a journey of two steps forward and one step back, you will begin to shape a new way of being by the messages you choose to give yourself. This is important.

A good way to understand the importance of this Gizmo is to read what some famous people have written about it and to regularly use the suggested messages you see in the Menu of Self-Talk on the next page.

Every man stamps his value on himself, man is made great or small by his own will.
~J. C. F. von Schiller

A man cannot be comfortable without his own approval. ~Mark Twain

What a man thinks of himself, that is what determines, or rather indicates, his fate.
~Henry David Thoreau

As soon as you trust yourself, you will know how to live. ~Johann von Goethe

If you hear a voice within you say 'you cannot paint' then by all means paint and that voice will be silenced. ~Vincent van Gogh

Like the sky opens after a rainy day we must open to ourselves. Learn to love yourself for who you are and open so the world can see you shine. ~James Poland

You have been criticizing yourself for years, and it hasn't worked. Try approving of yourself and see what happens. ~Louise Hay

You yourself, as much as anybody in the entire universe, deserve your love and affection. ~Buddha

MENU OF HIGH POWERED SELF-TALK

Create high powered self-talk based on what works for you and repeat constantly to overshadow the messages that haven't worked for years. Or choose from the options below.

An Empowering Quote
Choose a quote that empowers you. Review it as often as you can remember to. Make it part of your Reminder Ritual—it has the power to shift your existence.

"I Can't Wait to See What I'll Come Up with Next."
This is a phrase filled with joy, optimism, and a set up for a good time. What if you woke up saying this phrase every morning? Imagine the feeling of joy and its ability to catalyze creative expression.

"So What—I'll Do it Anyway."
A delightfully satisfying line that works when the inner critic or diabolical outer-world forces seem to be saying something dispiriting.
For instance: If you are under the influence of messages like: "You're too old," "You're not good enough," "Others have already done this, what if I'm wasting my time?" Neutralize them and energize defiant action by saying, "So what–I'll do it anyway."

"So?" (Related to the above phrase but pithier).
A saucy retort that refuses to take life so seriously. Helpful when the perfectionist in you gets overly serious about your work or when your highly sensitive nature is whiplashed by your deep reactions to the world. Try saying: "So?"
• Things aren't going perfectly . . . . So?
• I feel awkward learning something new and not being perfect at it . . . . So?
• I thought I'd be further along in this project by now . . . . So?
• Not everyone likes what I'm doing . . . . So?
• I got purple paint on my favorite white T-shirt . . . . So?
"So?" has a defiant attitude woven into it that comes in handy when rebelling against any message, thought, or outer force that tries to thwart your efforts.

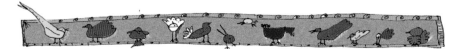

"It's Close Enough."

What to say to yourself when you've worked on something and want to practice being happy with it after a reasonable amount of effort rather than never being satisfied (or insidious perfectionism torment). Just say, "Close enough," to stave off the not-good-enough beast.

"I am on my own journey and doing things in my own time."

If you have overactive comparison-software in your brain, you can derail yourself by comparing yourself, your possessions, and your skills to others. Comparison is toxic to the creative process, but if you catch yourself doing it, be compassionate because comparison is unmistakably human. When you notice yourself comparing, consider gently wiping the slime off yourself and replying, "Hey, ya' know what? I am on my own journey, going at my own pace and am grateful for all I have done and all I have." And for extra credit add: "Plus, my wildly quirky process brings ME joy . . . and THAT's what I'm going for anyway." "Just stop it," sometimes works, too.

"I can do this."

This is a deliciously simple phrase that can be much more fun and helpful to say to ourselves than "I can't do this." "I can do this" is like fuel for perseverance. If it's too hard for you to believe, practice believing it just 5% more each time, or feel that it's true for just 15 seconds. Imagine what it might be like if it were true, or pretend you are someone who believes it.

Patience

Here is a lovely quartet of phrases to choose from when your impatience flares up:

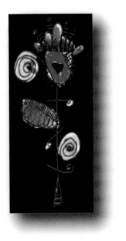

- "Okay, I'll put this down for a while."
- "I'll take a deep breath in and let go of the need to be impatient. It's all unfolding just the way it needs to."
- "Oh, good, I get to practice my patience. It will come in handy for JUST ABOUT EVERYTHING."
- "Oh look, a hummingbird" (i.e. distract yourself from the source of your impatience).

You may feel like dwelling on your limits or your fears. Don't do it. A perfect prescription for a squandered, unfulfilled life is to accommodate self defeating feelings while undercutting your finest, most productive ones. ~Marsha Sinetar

PROCESS FUEL

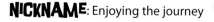

NICKNAME: Enjoying the journey

DESCRIPTION:

Set your intention to feel a certain way while you are engaged in the process. Instead of defaulting to tension and pressure when working creatively, decide to feel different, and the process will shift into a place of joy that keeps you coming back.

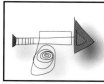

INDICATIONS FOR USE:

Set an intention of how you want to feel in the process of creating.

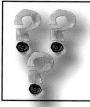

SUGGESTED QUESTIONS:

What do I want to feel in the creative process?
What feeling can I include in the present that I enjoyed in my creative process in the past?

APPLICABLE QUOTATIONS:

Painting is just a tool; it is nothing in itself. What counts is how you do it. ~Michele Cassou

I want to feel good about me in every step I take . . . I don't want to have to wait for the outcome to feel good. ~Dawn Kotzer

EXPLANATION

Describe how you want to feel in the creative process. (See next page for examples of combining feelings to elicit an intended state.) Allow the words to describe a feeling that is enticing and powers up the inspiration you need in order to get started and persevere. When you fuel your creative actions and intentions like this, the process takes on a whole new quality, one where you can merge with the present moment's higher feeling of enlightenment and discovery.

As Robert Henri says,

> The object isn't to make art, it's to be in that wonderful state which makes art inevitable.

Ideas spring from action

Make the action enjoyable

FUEL YOURSELF INTO LOVING THE PROCESS:
CHOOSE A COMBINATION OF WORDS THAT DESCRIBE HOW YOU WANT TO FEEL WHILE YOU CREATE

- playful anticipation
- fascinated presence
- child-like openness
- focus
- loving simplicity
- irreverent amusement
- calm magnificence
- flowing effortlessness
- mischievous amusement
- relaxed ease
- raucous delight
- delighted curiosity
- wild abandon
- conspired joy
- alert to discovery
- light wonder
- quiet trust

- audacious whimsicality
- liberated exhilaration
- unfettered belief
- loving focus
- open-eyed gratitude
- grateful observation
- graceful reflection
- intuitive listening
- conspired genius
- constant wonder
- frivlous play
- amused attention
- concentrated madness
- as if it's a breeze
- unpredictable clever
- delicious abandon

- alert fascination
- deliberate awe
- amplified mystique
- anticipated delight
- mellow meandering
- spectacular freedom
- child-like curiosity
- liberated celebration
- eager observation
- willing wonder
- cherished play
- deliberate mirth
- elevated innocence
- beginner's mind
- radical acceptance
- spontaneous clarity
- make one up

INSTEAD OF FOCUSING ON HOW MUCH YOU CAN ACCOMPLISH, FOCUS ON HOW MUCH YOU CAN ABSOLUTELY LOVE WHAT YOU'RE DOING.
~LEO BABAUTA

FUEL

ITS ABOUT THE PROCESS

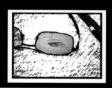

TAKING A BREAK

NICKNAME: BREAK!

DESCRIPTION:
Sometimes you need to step away from the process and take a break in order to reboot clarity, restore the faculties of resourcefulness, or simply to regain your sanity.

INDICATIONS FOR USE:
1. You are feeling overwhelmed.
2. You're experiencing Creative Chaos.
3. You seem to have brain-fog, are feeling nothing new is coming, are going around in circles, are writing the same line over and over, or are stuck in the same designs, colors, patterns, genre, or excuses.
4. You are frustrated.
5. You lose perspective and feel like what you're doing is crap.
6. When you've worked intensely for a period of time, at the end of a passionate expenditure of energy on a big project.

CONTRAINDICATIONS:
A revitalizing break feels like a breath of fresh air. Procrastination masquerading as a break has a deceptive feeling to it. When you are honest with yourself, you can feel the difference.

APPLICABLE QUOTATION:
It takes a lot of time to be a genius, you have to sit around so much doing nothing, really doing nothing. ~Gertrude Stein

RECOMMENDATIONS

• Take a Break. Breaks are especially effective right after you have immersed yourself in the process, have asked questions, and have explored and obsessed about a number of approaches. If you let go at this point, part of you is taking a break but you will be giving breakthroughs, new directions, or surges of insight a chance to happen. It's when you start thinking or doing something else that the ideas make themselves known.

• Trust that taking time away from your work is actually going to move you further along than if you stay in the process being all discombobulated and burnt out.
• A break is like rebooting your creativity.
• A break also gives insights the space to reveal themselves.

• Take a walk, a hike, a field trip, a vacation, go to Sea World, a bookstore, or an art gallery (gift shops in art museums work amazingly well). Float, waste some time on purpose, play, take a walk, a day off, expose yourself to something completely different, take a nap. (This book was written with at least 358 naps.)

• Take a drive and listen to really loud music or just listen to your thoughts.

• Read something completely unrelated to what you're doing. Or read a work by an author whose work revs up your creative engines.

• Experiment with and enlist other friends to take one whole day away from texting, clocks, iPads, computers, your cell phone, Facebook, Twitter, blogs, computer games. Be like a scientist studying your reaction and not only looking for, but expecting something refreshing.

Break-time

MEDITATION

NICKNAME: Calm reflection with a twist of imagination

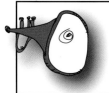

DESCRIPTION:
Quiet the incessant chatter of the mind, relax the body, and tap into a flow of inspiration, intuition, and imagination.

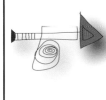

INDICATIONS FOR USE:
When you want creativity to flow from that inner reservoir of wisdom, connections, and grace that's usually obscured by mental chatter and fear.

ADDITIONAL OPERATING INSTRUCTIONS:
The mind has a tendency to disregard, avoid, or forget the power of being still and listening. so it requires fiery vigilance to fit meditation into your schedule. See Willingness, page 37. Ask yourself:
"How can I make it easier to find time for meditation?

SUGGESTED QUESTIONS:
1. When did a quiet mind yield a creative experience for me?
2. What would be a good time to regularly sit quietly and allow my muse to talk to me?
3. What experiences feel meditative?

RECOMMENDATIONS

Roaring dreams take place in a perfectly silent mind. ~Jack Kerouac

 Long intensive training in faraway caves with robed masters is not required to effectively quiet the mind. Just five minutes in the morning or before your creative time can clear a space for amazing insight and idea generation, but it takes practice. Longer periods of time practiced regularly will gift you with a steady delivery of creative enlightenment.

• If the term "meditation" conjures up anything but something inviting, call it something else: Relaxing, Reflection, and Expectancy; The Inner Connection; Grace; I Get to Be Quiet; Freedom From Chatter; Just Being; Free-floating Bliss; Reunion with Creative Spirit and Imaginative Wonder; Harriet; Rafael, whatever works for you. Apply gentle mindfulness without feeling hurried or under pressure.

• Meditation puts your brain into an alpha state, and when you practice enough, a waking theta state where creative ideas flow freely without mental censorship. With enough practice you can visit meditation as if you were entering a room filled with ideas and intuition.

• **How**: Get comfortable, take your time relaxing your body, and begin to feel the intoxication that can happen when you simply breathe. Quiet your thoughts, which for some of us will be for about four seconds. This is normal, don't give up. Just keep gently and lovingly redirecting your mind to your breathing and the place where creative possibility dwells inside of you. Counting backwards from 15 can structure your gradual acceptance of stillness. Don't expect it to be a perfect experience; at first it may be a parade of distractions, feeling lost in space, unaware that your rambling thoughts just took over again. The more you patiently practice and open to your inner wisdom, the more meditation will be an amazing resource for your creativity and peace of mind.

BE A KID

NICKNAME: Play

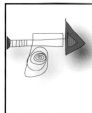

DESCRIPTION:

- A kid-like mind set helps you have fun AND succeed with creativity.
- Fun attracts interest, participation, and commitment. It gives you permission to let down a guard that can prevent the freedom to experiment.
- Playing with concepts and ideas is vital to discovery.
- Many silly ideas have turned into ingenious methods and products.

INDICATIONS:

Play oils the process with mischievous ingenuity; it shuns perfectionism, and cajoles scared brilliance out of hiding. If you use Kid-Stuff frequently, you will more freely express your creativity and ingenuity.

APPLICABLE QUOTATIONS:

"Play is the royal road to childhood happiness and adult brilliance." ~Joseph Chiltern Pearce

"The creative adult is the child who has survived."
~ Ursula K. Le Guin

SUGGESTED QUESTIONS:

- How can you remain childlike in the interest of your Creative Adventure?
- How can you make your Creative Adventure fun?
- What if this challenge was a game?

RECOMMENDATIONS

Those who shun the whimsy of things will experience rigor mortis before death.
~Tom Robbins

If your kid-like spirit is active, creativity will come more easily to you. Resistance often arises from taking things too seriously, putting too much pressure on yourself, and not making your Creative Adventure fun.

Nurturing our kid-likeness means we are nurturing agelessness, optimism, curiosity, uninhibitedness, experimentation, good humor, and aspects of our personality that motivate creative action and ideas.

THINK OF WAYS TO MAKE YOUR ENDEAVOR FUN:
• Instead of having a to-do list, make an "I get to . . ." list and notice your energy shift from the dread of a pressured adult to the eagerness of an animated child. Make your goals sound fun so you'll WANT to do them.

• Play doodle, scribble, have your Creative Adventure write to you. Replace the word "work" with "play" if it conjures up a lighter approach to things you want to get done:

• Kids like to come up with fun names. Name your Creative Adventure,-naming it makes it funner.

• Brainstorm other ways to make the project more fun: Use perspective, exaggeration, get big, get small, take it for a walk, discuss it with a fun friend, use fun media, do it in a fun place, etc.

• Take festive field trips just for the fun of it to make the kid-like spirit inside of you happy--you'll notice that your resistance decreases.

• Use permission slips: I give myself permission to make things up as I go along.

• Use rewards but do not underestimate the power of simply telling yourself: LOOK what YOU did!

• Have a creative intention in mind but allow the spontaneity of the child to decide what step he or she wants to choose next; a different intuitive energy will take over..

• Whenever possible make your creativity a game. Find fun people and groups who make it easy to play. Dare to take an improv comedy class.

REMINDERS

NICKNAME: "Oh yeah, that."

DESCRIPTION: We are truly our own sages, muses, and oracles. We have vast reservoirs of wisdom, answers, and profound understandings. But because we have a mind that often focuses on what we DON'T know, we forget how much we do. Remind yourself what works.

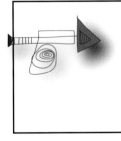

INDICATIONS FOR USE:
1. Right before starting something new.
2. When returning to something you put down for awhile.
3. In the middle of being stuck.
4. When feeling down about yourself.
5. And when wanting to remember that you have solved many problems and accomplished many things.

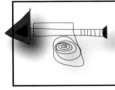

COUNTRAINDICATIONS:
Reminding yourself about old patterns, thoughts, and habits that don't work is not a good use of this Gizmo. Knock it off.

STANDARD QUESTIONS:
▶ What worked in the past when I got stuck with a challenge similar to the one I'm experiencing now?
▶ What's working now?
▶ How can I remember what works?
▶ Did I turn off the stove?

61

EXPLANATION

In order to stay alive back when we first walked the earth in the early Birkenstock® period, we would constantly ask, "What's wrong with this picture?" If we didn't consider what was amiss, boulders would fall on our heads, we would step on multistriped snakes, or be carried off by inconsiderate prehistoric birds. We still have to look both ways before crossing the street but we are not in the same dire physical danger as way back then, so we can start paying attention to what's right with us instead of what's wrong.

You will feel empowered and ready for firing on all your creative cylinders if you remind yourself of all that you have already overcome and what worked. Review your past where you got through challenges, REMEMBER what worked and apply it to your present Creative Adventure. And if nothing worked in the past or the solution wasn't the best, ask, "What ELSE might work?" Remember you can be amazingly strong when you tap into your power.

How will you remember what works for you? Once you finish reading your Owner's Manual you will have a myriad of tools from which to draw that will propel you into highly operational creativity. How will you remember to use them?

WAYS TO REMEMBER:

 A Creativity Realignment Journal: Collect reminders of what works, quotes, and images that remind you of your strengths and inspirations. It doesn't have to be fancy, just functional. Use one of those blank books on your shelf.

Place notes in pockets, drawers, cabinets, and inside shoes.

Send yourself an e-card, setting the delivery date for one month, two months, even a year from now.

Take your calendar, online or hard copy, and write reminders on days in the future.

Take turns with a friend, reminding each other of what works–write reminder duty dates on a calendar.

 Make a collaged, painted, or crayoned picture of your reminders.

Memorize what works, repeat it until it's an effortless habit.

WARM UPS
PERCOLATOR QUESTIONS
RAW MATERIALS
BEING ABSURD
THINKING CAPS
THE SUBCONSCIOUS

Associate • Modify • Pretend

WARMING UP

When the creative valve is stuck shut, try oiling it with warm-ups that provide quick successes. Success feels good and inspires more participation, and if you add perseverance, you soon find yourself gaining in a momentum-a very good place to be.

WAYS TO WARM UP YOUR CREATIVITY
Floundering
A wander
Freewriting
Alphabet associations
Exposure to cool things you've done before
Exposure to someone else's cool stuff that fires up your own butt
Scribbling, doodling, and play
Haiku
Acronyms and acrostics
Word Pools

FLOUNDERING
Floundering at the beginning of a creative endeavor is normal, but it is during moments of wondering where and how to start, feeling uncomfortable with the "not knowing," that you will easily fall prey to distractions. If you stay with the "flounder," (also known as a bottom-feeder fish), and NOT feed on the bottom but instead stay dedicated to making it through into a focused concentration, you are actually building skills that will help you persevere not only with your Creative Adventure, but in other areas of your life as well. The reward you get when you sink into the creative process is that feeling of finally being home after enduring a frustrating initiation of sorts.

GO FOR A WANDER WITH A SMALL QUESTION
Walking paired with paying attention has been a fertile channel for creative greats throughout the ages. If your mind is in multitasking mania it may not cooperate with focusing on one singular question, so begin by going for 15-second periods of focus at a time on the question. Your mind will begin to feel what it's like to stay focused, which will start to melt resistance. Just know it's normal for your mind to bounce around if you're out of practice and gently bring it back over and over (and over and over) to a small question. Coming back will be easier if it's a fun question.

FREEWRITING

Be a scribe for the spontaneous flow of thoughts coming through you. Don't judge, censor, or even punctuate. When you liberate yourself on the page, brilliance often slips in as a way of your muse saying thank you for not being a ruthless hard-ass. Some days it works, some days it doesn't … so experiment.

THE ALPHABET

Use the alphabet to stimulate a flow of ideas. You can start with a variety of subjects, from titles of poems, to places (literal and figurative) where you've lived. Use the letters of the alphabet as the first letter. Your list can then be Raw Materials for titles, stories, art ideas, photography, and unexpected ideas.

Example:

Places I've been (literal, figurative, off-the-wall)

Aware

Bahamas

Carnivals

Deli Llama (a delicatessen in my hood)

Everglades

Florida

Gainesville

Hammocks--wide variety, one kinda flimsy

I forget some places

Jill--been here all my life

Keep going with the rest of the alphabet.

This warm-up yielded me some ideas for writing, essays, and art. Next step: Spend five minutes starting something, mind-mapping, listing, or springing off into spontaneous merriment.

EXPOSURE TO COOL THINGS YOU'VE DONE BEFORE

Returning to favorite past accomplishments can power up the same energy that created them in the first place. Flip through writing, art, journals, finished projects you love. Entice yourself to add just one more sentence, brush stroke, image in slow motion to an unfinished project.

EXPOSURE TO THE WORK OF OTHERS

Reading works from your favorite authors, viewing art that inspires you, or exploring any creative endeavor that gets your juices flowing can jump-start you into action. In the process of doing this, ask small questions about how you might modify, do something similar with your own twist, and find associations that loosely or literally set you on your own course.

SCRIBBLING, DOODLING, AND PLAY

Self-explanatory.

HAIKUS

Haikus provide a short dose of creative satisfaction that can give a feeling of success, and success is fuel for necessary perseverance. Limited to just a few words, haikus still paint a vivid picture, elicit emotions, and provide that all important feeling of completing something. They contain your expectations and eliminate the feeling that you need to do more.

Here are two ways you can write haikus:

1. The classic way is a three-line poem. First line is five syllables, second one is seven syllables, and the third is five syllables. For example:

Life wrinkles when worn,
nothing is permanent press
wrinkle it deeply.

2. The second way is five lines. First line is one word, second is two words, third is a sentence of any reasonable length, fourth is two words, and fifth is one word.

Fall
Leaves tumble
And pile in mounds of warm, autumn colors.
Go ahead.
Jump.

ACRONYM AND ACROSTICS

Like the alphabet, starting with letters to stimulate words is a good brain warm-up.
An acryonym uses one word per letter:

Weaving
Otherworldly
Rowdy
Delight

And an acrostic uses any number of words you need per letter:

White morning dawn calls to the
Osprey, floating effortlessly on
Reaches of sky
Deliberating over its prey below.

Not sure how this cupake got here. Yours!

WORD POOLS

Collections of words and phrases chosen randomly make for easy assembly when you add more and let them take you on a journey. You'll find several word pools in the Day-to-Day Maintenance Datebook. Try one now using some or all of these words and adding more as you need them: run, believe, cupboard, stairs, corners, cries, branches, ultimate, holding, hundreds, must be done, fades, time, real.

Andre climBs to
the moon
and Back
everyday...
Because he's
GOING through
a phase.

CAPTIONS AND TINY STORIES

Make up funny little captions for photos or illustration or 1- to 3-line stories.
Not only is it a good way to warm up, the stories you write are precious little mirth makers in and of themselves.

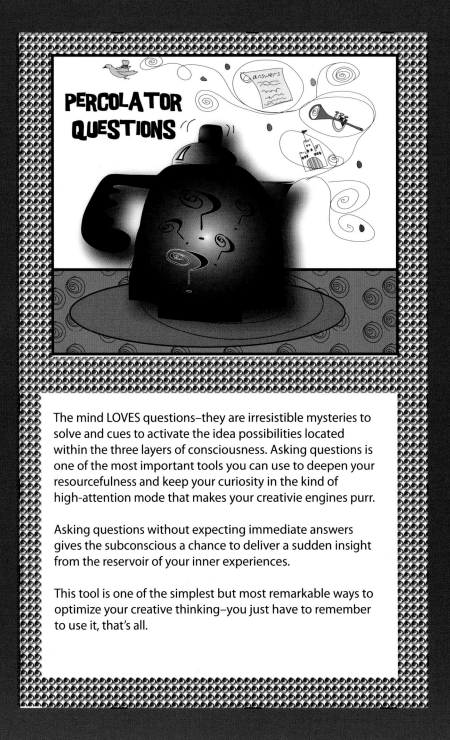

PERCOLATOR QUESTIONS

The mind LOVES questions–they are irresistible mysteries to solve and cues to activate the idea possibilities located within the three layers of consciousness. Asking questions is one of the most important tools you can use to deepen your resourcefulness and keep your curiosity in the kind of high-attention mode that makes your creativie engines purr.

Asking questions without expecting immediate answers gives the subconscious a chance to deliver a sudden insight from the reservoir of your inner experiences.

This tool is one of the simplest but most remarkable ways to optimize your creative thinking–you just have to remember to use it, that's all.

ASKING PERCOLATOR QUESTIONS WILL:

- Get the mind into a habit of generating answers, ideas and wonder.
- Dislodge thinking from repetitive-thinking loops into active idea finding.
- Disarm creative resistance that comes from the demanding inner critic.
- Optimize the creative zone of searching for more than one solution.
- Set your observation radar for finding connections, associations, and aha moments.
- Shift you from victim to mastery; e.g. from, "I'm stuck, I can't do this," to: "What worked for me in the past?" "What will work?" "How cool am I?"

CONTRAINDICATIONS:

Pay attention to the questions you ask yourself. The mind will also find answers to questions like, "Why are other people so far ahead of me?" "Why don't I ever finish anything?" or "Why am I such a nincompoop?" The answers to these questions will not serve you as much as "How will seeing the work of others inspire my next tiny step?" "How would it feel to be kind to myself for a change?" or "What will inspire me today?"

EXAMPLES OF PERCOLATOR QUESTIONS:

- If focusing on my creativity were a top priority, what small things would I be thinking and doing now?
- What tiny small thought can I think to get myself inspired about my creative project?
- What one small way can I make my writing/art/music/life fresh?
- What interesting thing will the character in my book do next?
- How can I make this a little more uniquely me?
- How can I make getting to my creative pursuit a little easier?
- What is this trying to say?
- Who inspires me and what would it feel like to imagine their energy motivating me?
- What would it feel like to have a relaxed, mischievous focus on my creative project?
- What would it feel like to believe in myself?
- Am I asking questions in a way that serves me?
- How will I remember to ask these kinds of questions?
- Would it make a difference to ask them with an Irish accent?

USE RAW MATERIALS:

to Free-Associate, List, and
Mind-Map

to Modify Existing Ideas

to Keep Going with Lines,
Quotes, and Titles

The vast, shiny whiteness of the blank page, the canvas, or the mind (which also comes in shades of gray), is enough to stump even the most experienced Creative Adventurer. Raw Materials make slipping into creative motion simpler by providing you with someting that you can then turn into something else. Creativity comes from making associations and connections, and toying with convergences of thoughts; seeing things in a new way–extrapolating, expounding, and using different perspectives that allow new concepts to be seen.

All those processes begin with preexisting material that triggers new ideas.

Raw Materials are words, images, objects, concepts, structures, and other stimuli already in existence that give you a place to start and banish the bewilderment of blankness. Raw Materials seduce you to take something in your own unique direction by rearranging, modifying, using an aspect of, repackaging, tweaking, springing off of it, and adding your personal twist: These actions are some of the most effective ways of being creative.

Many creative greats don't use anything BUT associating and modifying from Raw Materials, so don't think you're cheating by not starting from scratch. On the next few pages you will be shown how Raw Materials, in their various forms, are used to easily start your creative engines running the direction of new ideas.

Everything is raw material. Everything is relevant. Everything is usable. Everything feeds into my creativity. But without proper preparation, I cannot see it, retain it, and use it.
~Twyla Tharp

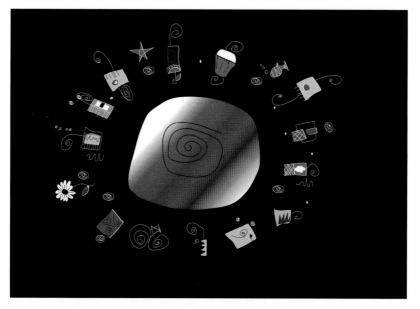

USE RAW MATERIALS TO FREE ASSOCIATE

Start with an image, word, sentence, object, or an existing concept and let it send you into a fluid fury of idea generation. Think of anything it loosely reminds you of, the opposite of it, what it sounds like, and what objects, pictures, concepts, ideas, stories, directions, wildness, tameness relate to it.

Don't judge, be crazy-on-fire, snarl, drool, and hum loudly if that helps. Wax otherworldly, be unpredictable, ridiculous. Channel the radically possessed populace of liberated artists/writers who were charmed with fierce independence. Do not impede a wild stampeding charge of associations. You might land on one response that completely rocks your world, circle it, but consider continuing because you may be surprised at how much brilliance, humor, and richness can emerge when you insist on going deeper.

At any given moment the brain is automatically forming new
associations, continually connecting an everyday x to an unexpected y.
~Jonah Lehrer

WAYS TO FREE-ASSOCIATE

JUST START BLABBING: It works better than no blabbing.

LIST: The fluid listing of ideas, possibilities, and answers actually forges new brain pathways making future idea-accessibility easier. Listing instructs your subconscious to continue working on finding responses even after you stop. Regular listing will support you in being naturally resourceful.

MIND-MAP: Mind-mapping works in the same nonlinear fashion that the mind works. You branch off from a central idea into any and every association and then those ideas branch off into more ideas or connect to existing ones.

Mind maps help generate, visualize, structure, and classify ideas, organize information, solve problems, and make decisions without being limited to listing in one direction.

Once you've finished mind-mapping, the results might look like one big overwhelming, scrawled mess. The process itself is important for discovery of new ideas and will leave you more enlightened, but the trick using what you've created, is to zone in on what within the mind map results energizes you the most. Or just paint a watercolor wash over the whole thing and frame it.

LIST OR MIND-MAP ASSOCIATIONS TO THESE WORDS:

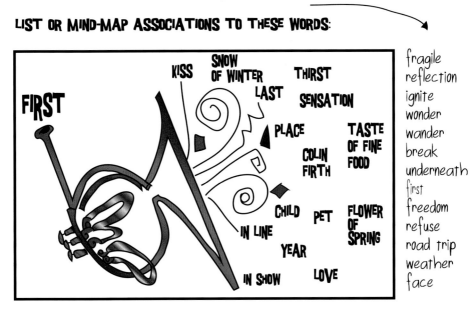

FIRST

KISS
SNOW OF WINTER
THIRST
LAST
SENSATION
PLACE
TASTE OF FINE FOOD
COLIN FIRTH
CHILD
PET
FLOWER OF SPRING
IN LINE
YEAR
IN SHOW
LOVE

fragile
reflection
ignite
wonder
wander
break
underneath
first
freedom
refuse
road trip
weather
face

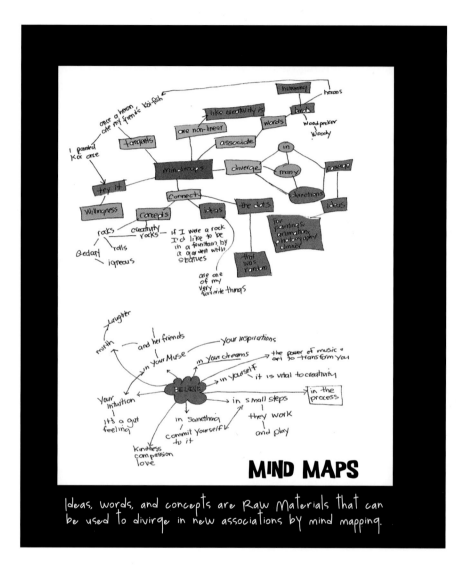

MIND MAPS

Ideas, words, and concepts are Raw Materials that can be used to divirge in new associations by mind mapping.

MODIFY

One of the most successful creative devices for generating ideas and innovation, is to start with an idea that is already in existence as your Raw Material. Tweak, modify, add, cut, and redo it so that it has your spin. Combine it with other ideas. Creative greats like Steve Jobs and William Shakespeare modified existing structures to forge into their wild successes by adding their own stamp of originality.

What ideas already in existence can you modify? Be on the lookout for what and how you can adapt, rearrange, and tweak existing ideas, concepts, visuals, systems, products, and instructions.

Pay attention to everything you encounter and ask yourself, "How can this relate to my creative idea?"

OBJECTS

Fluency of thought is further developed when you take an object and list everything it reminds you of or what else it could be used for—logically or illogically. This kind of practice will develop the skill of idea fluency which leads to creative resourcefulness.

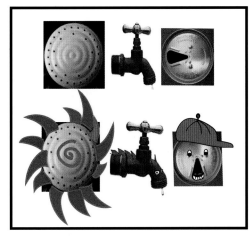

This could be:
a ring
a miniature vase
a toothpick holder
an earring
an alien
a percussion instrument
a mini telescope
a viewfinder for your next tiny step
What else?

KEEP GOING WITH RAW MATERIALS:

Use lines, titles, quotes that other people have come up with as Raw Materials to spring off of.

Writer's block is a fancy term made up by whiners so they can have an excuse to drink alcohol. You can safely use up to three sentences of someone else's work—unless you're friends, then two . . .

The odds of being found out are very slim, and even if you are there's usually no jail time.

~Steve Martin

PLAY WITH CONTINUING WITH THESE LINES:

One summer afternoon Mrs. Oedipa Maas came home from a Tupperware party . . .
~Thomas Pynchon, The Crying of Lot 49

Gerald Maines lived across the hall from a woman named Benna, who four minutes into any conversation always managed to say… ~Lorrie Moore, Anagrams

For a long time, I went to bed early. ~Marcel Proust, Swann's Way

There was a time when . . .
Maybe the world is . . .
Would it make a difference . . .
If you have never . . .
She just wants to be . . .
The garden is mumbling something . . .
I like the way . . .
I was just thinking about . . .
There was only seven minutes left . . .

If I took my thoughts . . .
Why do I . . .
For years and years . . .
Here is the . . .
Leave the . . .
Turn the . . .
I won't be . . .
It's not what you think, it's . . .
As soon as you . . .

The Day-to-Day Maintenance Datebook is filled with Raw Materials for you to play with. Open to any page for practice. Feel mischievously rebellious and do a June prompt in February. Return to the same prompts over and over—your responses will change, your creativity will deepen.

BE ABSURD

Some stories are true that never happened. ~Elie Weisel

Only those who attempt the absurd... will achieve the impossible. ~M.C. Escher:

SUSPEND LOGIC

Scoffing at what seems illogical is what skeptics throughout history have done with blind ignorance at ridiculous things like the car, the TV, the phone, and the movies. Is that the crowd you want to be associated with? Sure, absurd notions that actually turn into something grand are not the rule, but the permission to suspend logic and consider the ridiculous is good creative sense and can possibly lead to ingenuity.

BREAK RULES

As soon as you get caught up in whether you are following rules correctly, you deny your intuitive creative compass its ability to lead you to guidelines that come from an authentic place versus a compliant one. Directions were invented by people who put in writing ONE way to do something–it's not the only way. You can use other people's directions as a starting place or as Raw Materials. You veer off into a more satisfying and unique process when you change the directions to fit your instincts. It doesn't always require extra thought; sometimes it's as easy as following an impulse that makes sense to your particular frame of view. The world of academia rewarded us when we followed directions; the world of creative innovation will praise you when you make up your own. Terrify your inner critic with bold creative actions that defy the conventional and confuse the conformers. Baffle your insecurity by letting go of what others think even if you just start a little bit.

Being absurd can transport one's mind out of the mundane and the trip can refresh a brain into seeing beyond the habitual.

You can't always write a chord ugly enough to say what you want to say, so sometimes you have to rely on a giraffe filled with whipped cream. ~Frank Zappa

THINKING CAPS

My destination is no longer a place, rather a new way of seeing.
~Marcel Proust

People should think things out fresh and not just accept conventional terms and the conventional way of doing things. ~R. Buckminster Fuller

How would approaching your Creative Adventure be different if you acted as if you were: the go-to expert, a bandit, a crazy person, a trickster, someone who pays no attention to detail, a detail-nut, a kid, a movie director, a hillbilly? How about calibrating your approach from: the feeling of grace, acceptance, or grandiosity, or the genre of mystery, adventure, or romantic comedy? What new products, inventions, events, stories, or projects would you come up with if you thought with a new perspective? Take a moment to muse about this.

Thinking Caps challenge you to tap into all the possibilities inside of you that get disregarded when you automatically settle for your first response, your default mode, or the obvious. Seeing from a different view will direct you to variations on themes, modifications of ideas, and to the coveted place of constant cleverness.

Pick a topic to test-drive. If you can't think of one, get a sense of how Thinking Caps work by playing with me as I use "windows" as a subject to trigger ideas for writing or art. See my responses (over on the right). They show how I would think of windows if I wore a few different Thinking Caps. Keep going by choosing new angles from which to see windows from the list over there on the right or come up with your own responses to all of them. Go beyond the ideas I came up with. It helps to actually wear a hat or two when you're doing this but that's optional. (Different hair-dos work as well.)

Act as if you are a genius and consider your imperfections a statement of the genre you unapologetically exemplify.

THINKING CAPS, SUBJECT: WINDOWS

Feisty: Write about yelling gutsy things out the window at people passing.

Childlike: Write about childhood memories about looking out the window of a car waiting for mom.

Compulsive: Write about not being able to concentrate because there's a smudge on the window or having to have the curtains hang exactly "right."

Erotic: Write or render art about looking into other people's windows or dressing in front of a window.

Actor: Write about acting in front of a window or in its reflection or act like a window.

Enlightened: Write or render art about the window of the soul.

Reckless: Write about throwing something and breaking a window.

Magical: Write or render art about a window that opens to something different each time it's opened.

Empty: Write or render art about a window looking into an empty room.

Associative: Write about looking through Microsoft Windows and seeing error messages.

THINKING CAPS: ACT AS IF YOU ARE . . .

adaptive	driven	meddling	the boss
audacious	eager	overzealous	an alien
brave	easy	paranoid	a bus boy
childlike	eccentric	peculiar	a foreigner
clumsy	edgy	perplexed	a director
compassionate	elated	playful	an actor
comfortable	elegant	reckless	a comedienne
compulsive	empowered	relieved	a scientist
cool	erotic	savvy	a monk
courageous	fascinated	secretive	a diva
cowardly	feisty	snooty	your favorite person
cranky	festive	soft	a creative genius
crazy	free-spirited	stubborn	a child prodigy
creative	glib	superstitious	a flamboyant artist
cunning	haunting	tricky	a spy
curious	helpful	triumphant	a favorite movie character
cynical	hip	talkative	a tour guide
demanding	humble	tame	a goddess
devoted	idealistic	truthful	a believer
disgusted	imaginative	under a spell	a talk-show host
disobedient	ingenious	unpredictable	a fish
distracted	magical	versatile	any animal
		(add your own)	a muse

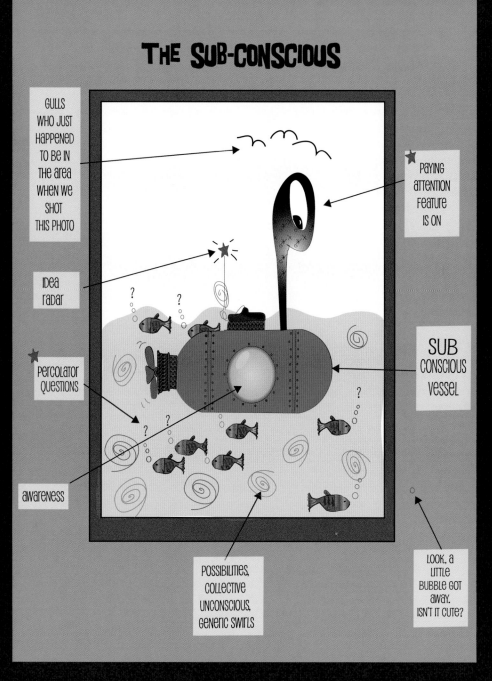

THE SUB-CONSCIOUS

GULLS WHO JUST HAPPENED TO BE IN THE AREA WHEN WE SHOT THIS PHOTO

PAYING ATTENTION FEATURE IS ON

IDEA RADAR

PERCOLATOR QUESTIONS

SUB CONSCIOUS VESSEL

AWARENESS

POSSIBILITIES, COLLECTIVE UNCONSCIOUS, GENERIC SWIRLS

LOOK, A LITTLE BUBBLE GOT AWAY. ISN'T IT CUTE?

USING YOUR SUB-CONSCIOUS

There are two main ways you can use your Sub-conscious settings for your creativity:

1 Turn the **Paying Attention** and **Asking Percolator Questions** features to the HIGH setting (i.e. be paying attention and asking lots of good questions as often as you can). Your Idea Radar will then be calibrated to notify you when ideas emerge. It may take time so be patient, but it may happen immediately as well. Take notes!

2 Aim your **intention** in the direction you want to go, but then distract yourself with something mindless like showering, driving, or dusting your collection of porcelain penguins, and notice that when you direct your attention elsewhere, ideas float up to your consciousness. Take more notes!

FUEL YOUR SUBCONSCIOUS BY HAVING LOTS OF DIFFERENT EXPERIENCES, READING, RESEARCHING, DREAMING, BEING CURIOUS, AND EXPOSING YOURSELF TO THOSE THINGS THAT INSPIRE YOU.

TROUBLE-SHOOTING GUIDE

Every time you meet a situation you think at the time is an impossibility and you go through the tortures of the damned, once you have met it and lived though it, you find that forever after you are freer than you ever were before.
~Eleanor Roosevelt

THE TROUBLESHOOTER KA*2500 *(KA= Kick "Butt")

TROUBLESHOOTING THE FOLLOWING:

1. Creative Chaos
2. Resistance and Rebellion
3. Fear
4. Perfectionism
5. Overwhelmed
6. Ruthless Self-Talk
7. Self-Sabotage
8. Procrastination

ISSUE: CREATIVE CHAOS

Chaos pictured is smaller than actual size.

DESCRIPTION:

You start a creative adventure of any type and run into a gigantic roadblock.
You keep starting projects but don't finish them.
You can't figure out how to bring the idea in your mind into reality.

WHAT YOU'RE THINKING:

I don't know what to do next, I'm confused, bewildered, and hungry.
This is too hard; I guess I don't have what it takes to do this.
What the . . . . ?

NORMALIZE THE EXPERIENCE:

Creative chaos is a normal part of the process. Refrain from blaming it on
some skill, aptitude, or wisdom that you lack.

VARY YOUR APPROACH

Creativity is organic and not static, so what works one day, may not work another. Try different approaches and attitudes. Listen to different music.

ASK YOURSELF:

~How can I best relax and just let the process be what it is until some little thread of clarity pops up and pulls me in? ~What might work for me? Allow the question to percolate. If you get answers to those questions, plot their instigation. ~What idea is going to show up and direct my next step? Let it percolate.

TAKE A BREAK

Step away from the project. PUT THE PROJECT DOWN and no one gets hurt. Get some perspective, renew, refill, meditate, sit so still that your Muse can whisper sweet-somethings in your ear. Take a walk, a shower, a vacation. If that's what you need you'll get further by restoring your perspective than by tormenting yourself.

LOWER EXPECTATIONS

If taking a break doesn't work, allow yourself some justified floundering around in the process, knowing that flailing through it is better than giving up and often leads to a breakthrough.

BE DETERMINED

85% of Creative Adventurers quit at this stage. Be in the 15% that stay the course. Affirm this: Some little ray of light is going to enlighten a next step soon.

LIGHTEN UP

Play with and explore absurd solutions and ideas. Forge through the chaos with crazy and amused wildness. Remember that play is known for resulting in discoveries but if it doesn't, the worst that can happen is that you have fun, and fun will keep you in the process.

CHOOSE A DIFFERENT PERSPECTIVE

Think from a different point of view; borrow one from someone who has made it through dilemmas of this sort and use their power as your own. Be rebelliously devoted to solving the challenge—experiment with different approaches with intense perseverance, rising above frustration and simply observing what may work with scientific objectivity rather than emotional drama.

BREAK IT DOWN INTO REALLY TINY STEPS

and approach those steps like an observer of your own process, as if you are making a documentary and narrating how this interesting individual is getting through the chaos. Again, be like a scientist who is without attachment to drama, and just keep trying new things.

EXPOSE YOURSELF

to something inspiring simply to reboot. Stay gently alert for ways to reengage in the process.

REACH OUT

to someone safe who is on your wavelength. Talk to them about your ideas just to hear what you have to say. Talking aloud uses a different brain pathway where new insights come through. AVOID sharing your stuff with people who don't get you.

DESCRIPTION:

Rebellion comes naturally to creative souls in their quest to defy the norm and discover original ways to do things.

Nonconforming styles that deviate from rules often lead an individual into innovation and individualism. Unfortunately, that same rebellious dynamic can inconveniently come into play when the same individuals refuse to follow through with their own creative call.

WHAT YOU'RE THINKING:

You can't MAKE me work.

CHALLENGE:

You plan on engaging in your Creative Adventure and end up being stopped by massive amounts of stubborn resistance.

TROUBLESHOOTING DIRECTIONS:

➤ The inner kid is a major player in rebellion and resistance. Coax it into participation by making the adventure fun: Give your project a name, promise small rewards, pretend you're a character who is ruthlessly committed to your creativity.

➤ Rebel against procrastination. In other words, engage in what you've been putting off as an act of defiance.

➤ Resistance can be a subconscious dynamic that kicks in because you feel somewhere in your life you have felt unfairly treated. You may mistake the adult inside you for the ones who crossed you in the past, perhaps feeling like you are getting them back by not complying, but in reality you are punishing yourself. Break the pattern by taking gentle small steps as a gesture of self-love. Stop punishing yourself.

➤ Acknowledge that there were also influences in childhood, (both positive and negative), that led to some of your more brilliant behaviors. This will help you focus on being more willing to be on your own side rather than playing out resentment toward injustices by rebelling against yourself.

➤ Team up with a buddy and be working at the same time on different projects; take a class; be kinder to yourself.

➤ If all else fails, use steadfast determination to barrel through the gates of resistance into your creative process despite its efforts to deny your entry. Repeating this day after day will dwarf rebellion's ability to stop you. This is how many creative greats have accomplished amazing things. You can too.

The only way to deal with an unfree world is to become so absolutely free that your very existence is an act of rebellion.
~Albert Camus

Creativity is a beautiful form of rebellion.

ISSUE: FEAR

DESCRIPTION:

The creative process naturally brings up fears. It exposes who we are, it challenges our ego to persevere when we don't feel competent, it amplifies our insecurities, and demons from our past reemerge when we desire expression. Creativity is a process that pushes us to our edges; it has been vital to our survival and equated with our worth. Fear, therefore, is a normal part of the journey.

When Creative Adventurers persevere in spite of fear, they are rewarded with self-respect and courage, two attributes that pave the way for greater works of creativity.

THINGS YOU DO WHEN IN FEAR:

~Feel frozen.
~Wish you could do something creative but it just doesn't happen.
~Avoid your Creative Adventure by doing anything but it.
~You start a lot of projects so you don't have deal with the scary part of any of them.

  *Use the excuse of having too many ideas to choose from so you don't have to begin and face the fears.

  *Rationalize that you need to be there for others all the time.

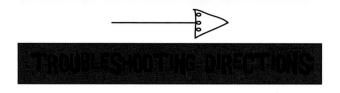

CONTROL YOUR FEARS

Write down all the fears you have related to the creative process. When they are in black and white on the page, you disarm their technicolor exaggeration.

EXPLORE YOUR PAST

Was there anywhere in your past where you felt fear, but persevered despite it? How did you do that? Can you do it again?

Apply a courageous moment from your past to the present moment mentally, spiritually, and physically.

BREAK IT DOWN

Shut off the fear center of your brain by lowering expectations and making each step so small there is no fear. Small steps will get you past the fear and into the flow, the momentum replaces fear, and you move further than if you try to take huge leaps. Any time you notice a new fear steering you away from your adventure (and you have to vigilantly pay attention, because they will sneak in when you're not watching), once again lower expectations, and take small steps, including the small step of simply imagining your next steps.

SHOOTING SPECIFIC FEARS

WHAT IF I'M NOT GOOD ENOUGH?

Practice begets confidence and skill. You're not supposed to be proficient at the beginning of an endeavor. Give yoursef permission to be a beginner. You can only get better in motion, with practice.

Highly accomplished creative people regularly admit that enjoying the process is the most important part of creativity. Savor the journey, decide on how you want to feel during it, decide what thought you want to think, and then let the results take care of themselves. (See Process Fuel on page 51.)

WHAT IF I FAIL?

When you hesitate because you fear failure, your action is based on unlived, unsubstantiated presumptions and not on real facts. What if you embodied the thoughts of those who know failing is just part of the process? Like:

"I failed my way to success." ~Thomas Edison

"Perseverance is failing nineteen times and succeeding the twentieth." ~Julie Andrews

Most wildly successful people know that failure is a normal part of the process. The first step is to be aware of the fear, the second is to ignore it.

WHAT IF I SUCCEED?

Usually this fear comes from dreading that there will be more pressure and responsibility with success, or not wanting to disappoint anyone, including yourself. To help remedy this, imagine what it would be like to feel relaxed and successful at the same time. Then decide to just expect tiny changes at the beginning. Be patient, this fear doesn't always change quickly but it does change when you're paying attention and being gentle. Suggested Self-Talk: "I can do this. Tiny steps and reasonable expectations will help me get used to this new way to feel."

WHAT IF I'M WASTING TIME AND MONEY FOR NOTHING?

Nothing is wasted if you embrace the beauty of the process. See Fringe Benefits on page 19.

Then again, what if I'm fabulous?

"Be Bold. It's just canvas, just paint. If it doesn't work for you, paint over it and start again. Don't be afraid that you are wasting supplies. Every failure teaches something, if only what not to do." ~Tiko Kerr

This goes for any endeavor, not just painting.

FEAR OF THINKING AN IDEA IS GREAT & FINDING OUT IT SUCKS.

Chalk it up as practice. Put it down for a while and come back to it. Often we forget what we were aiming for and when we return to it, it seems better than we thought. But not always, and in that case modify, practice, start over, move on, come back and repeat. This is part of the process.

FEAR OF ALIENATING FRIENDS OR SIGNIFICANT OTHERS

You will attract your believers, your tribe and your kindred friends when you're true to yourself. Being true to yourself will make you a better person for those around you.

FEAR THAT YOU'RE TOO OLD

Age is no barrier to the creative process.

Creativity has the potential to get better with age because of the life experiences you have to draw from, the inhibitions you give up, the inspiration that comes from acknowledging that life doesn't go on forever up, and the tendency to be enlightened as to what truly matters.

Falling in love with your creativity keeps you young more than almost anything else. You may not be a success in the classic sense, but definitions of success are up for modification because many of them don't result in happiness. Feeling creative joy and sharing your gifts is one of the most healthy definitions there is of success.

"I never feel age . . . If you have creative work, you don't have age or time."
~Louise Nevelson

MOVE THROUGH YOUR FEARS
"All art requires courage." ~Anne Tucker

Don't let the reality of others get in the way of YOUR dreams.

ISSUE:
PERFECTIONISM

THE TROUBLE:

Your creativity isn't running smoothly because you're immobilized or made it a stressful chore by unrealistically expecting yourself to be perfect.

With perfectionism:
You may equate your worth not with who you are, but with the quality and "success" of your work.

You may be sabotaging yourself because your standards are unrealistic and you assume they are.

You have made yourself captive to the judgments of others or to your own relentless self-evaluation.

There is often no joy in the process because there is so much pressure, comparison, judgment, and unrealistic thinking involved.

Even when something is well received by others, you still feel that it's not good enough. You focus almost exclusively on what is wrong, ignoring what's going right.

You may have a hard time tolerating not being competent even at the beginning of a project so you give up quickly or don't even begin to engage in the practice necessary to get better.

You think there's just one right way to do things and surrender your intuition to instructions someone else put together.

You value being faultless far too much in a process that thrives on exploring the potential of mistakes, imperfections, and blunders to be brilliant solutions, ingenious detours, and unexpectedly wonderful ideas.

Includes the wrong kind of paper, the muddy look of painting over paint before it dries, uneven lines, wobbly drawings, and mistakes. So? It was fun and freeing.

TROUBLESHOOTING DIRECTIONS:

➤ Relax your expectations, in fact, purposely lower them so low that you feel excitedly naughty about showing up to perform your work with reckless abandon. If that's hard, open to doing this notion just 5% more. Deliberately perform below your skill-level to get started and to see what ideas fall out of a relaxed approach.

➤ Approach your work with beginner's mind, like a child discovering the ever-new land of your Creative Adventure.

➤ Do not compare yourself with anyone and if you catch yourself, say this, "HEY! I'm not perfect . . . so I compared myself to someone, big deal. Okay, now that I got THAT out of system, I'm going revel about my own unique stengths."

➤ Considering having the intention of entertaining yourself as the chief reason you are having a Creative Adventure and know that's one of the philosophies used by enterprising creative giants.

➤ Get real. Being perfect just isn't possible within the realm of being human and those who strive to be perfect often sacrifice joy in the process. If you strive for "amazing" but let go of expectations and are happy with whatever results you reap, then you're on a healthier and more realistic path .

➤ Do you have any idea how much time you can free up if you stop trying to make things perfect all the time? It's time you can use for much more important things, plus allowing things to be "close enough" versus "perfect" is still often way above average for a perfectionist.

mistakes can become new design directions

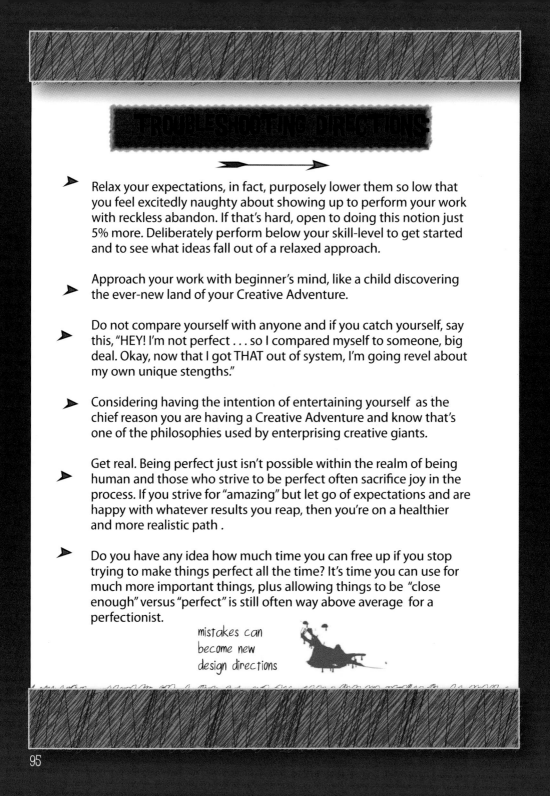

- Learn to give yourself credit. At first you will need to pretend that you can accept acknowledgement. Imagine what it would be like to truly accept that you are good enough. Just imagine.

- Don't beat yourself up for being imperfect about being uncomfortable with being imperfect.

- Let go of the "all or nothing at all" approach. Some of what you do will be fabulous, some will be okay, some will suck. That's the PROCESS, and that's life, relationships, work, and creativity.

- When you find yourself stressing on getting something perfect, try out the mantra, "Ah it's good enough."

- Learn to embrace compliments. Feel their power and believe they are true even if it's just a tiny bit more.

- Experiment with your process by going fast, setting a timer, getting into the process versus the product orientation. Use the Ready-Fire-Aim method!

- Imagine what it would be like to be one of those people who are reckless, imperfect, and wildly happy because they are NOT hung up on oppressive perfectionism. Hang out with them.

if done of these solutions work... act as if like they do and see what happens.

The feeling of piling up or spiraling out of your control
can create a feeling of helplessness and immobilization.
Feeling overwhelmed can cause creativity to go on the fritz.

COMMON OVERWHELMED THINKING:

"I need to do it all, be it all, right now, but there's so much and it's HARD. I don't have enough time, people are surpassing me, and it feels like I'm drowing."

DESCRIPTION:
~ Your thoughts, expectations, and life-dramas are out of control because you're trying to take on too much all at once or your perception is out-of-whack.
~ You feel unable to move, accompanied by a glazed look, sort of like a deer in headlights.
~ You might feel like crying.
~ You're a little unkempt; it's possible your shirt is buttoned incorrectly.

TROUBLESHOOTING DIRECTIONS:

Breathe (always a good thing and very low cost.) Notice how taking in five breaths at a time doesn't work. Use this to remind you to just focus on one tiny step at a time.

Break things way down. The first step can be as small as turning to face your desk. You can accomplish an amazing amount of what you want when you take small steps. Dive into the next very tiny step without a lot of thought. And you'll experience a lot of successes with tiny steps which fuels passion–an energy filled with the determination you need.

Allow yourself to approach your first step with compassion and curiosity. Let go of the need to be perfect. Perfectionism is a major cause of feeling overwhelmed. Go for "close enough."

Make a list of all that needs to be done. Often the overwhelm is worse when everything is swirling around in your head picking up debris like exaggeration, fear, and a slew of junk mail. You probably don't need to do everything on your list, really. Let some go.

Put "I get to" in front of each item on your list to shift from dread to eagerness. Eagerness will sustain you longer. Choose a priority. Make a list at the end of the day of everything you that "got to" do, including the things not on your list. You'll be fortified and pleasantly surprised by how much you did.

Take a break for clarity; take a walk, talk to a friend. Make it easy to show up. Decide that your process will be fueled by calm simplicity.

Lose the word "always," as in "I'm always overwhelmed." Chances are you are not ALWAYS overwhelmed, but using that word will increase your perception that you *are* and the probability that you *will be.*

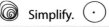 Simplify.

THE ANTI-OVERWHELM PERISCOPE

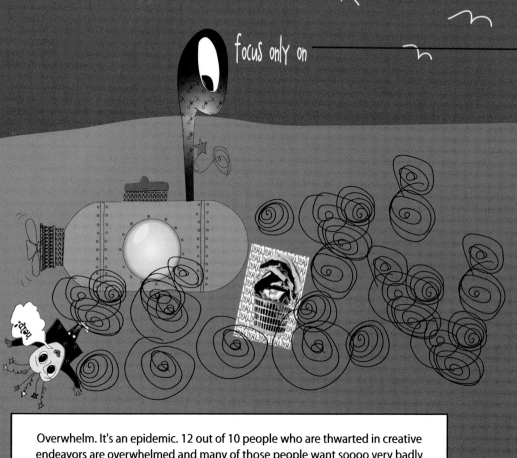

focus only on _____

Overwhelm. It's an epidemic. 12 out of 10 people who are thwarted in creative endeavors are overwhelmed and many of those people want soooo very badly to get TO their creative passion but instead are swirling in a cyclone of distractions, shoulds, and two more loads of whites.

Here are two imaginative devices to gently consider:

FIRST, try smiling at your overwhelm. I'll wait. No really, smile at your overwhelm. Notice any difference? If nothing else, it lightens you up a bit. Taking your creative work and your life too seriously is a significant part of being overwhelmed. Okay, if that just annoyed you, which would be understandable, hold on for the second one:

ACTIVATE YOUR ANTI-OVERWHELM PERISCOPE

Imagine yourself in a submarine moving through an ocean of all the ingredients of your overwhelm. Take a minute to make it real. Now imagine a periscope rising up above the surface of all that overwhelms you.
Let one small aspect of your creative endeavor come into view within that periscope. What is it? What would be fun to do with it?
Where and when will you do that for just 5 minutes?
Even just thinking about your creativie endeavor can create a wake of motivation.

Aim your attention in the direction of your one-small-aspect and as you glide effortlessly through the overwhelm, begin to imagine returning to the flow of your creative passion.

What's your favorite feeling when you're IN the flow? Write it down, close your eyes and feel it now for just 15 seconds.

Trust it's possible. Proceed.

ISSUE:

RUTHLESS SELF-TALK

blah blah blah blah blah blah blah blah blah blah blah blah blah

NINCOMPOOP   dUMb bUtt

Argue for your limitations, and sure enough, they're yours. ~Richard Bach

If you tell yourself that you are not good enough, you are too old, and it's too hard, you will act in accordance with these thoughts and make them true.

Here's what typically happens to your creativity in response to harsh self-talk. You will:
1. Discourage yourself and give up.
2. Succeed but feel very little joy in the process and with the results.
3. Be resistant in order to get back at yourself for being so mean.
4. Be chronically cranky, envious, and wrinkle easily.

Changing your self-talk if it's not working for you is one of the biggest creative gifts you can give to yourself, but it requires practice.
Your consciousness does not change with the simple realization that there is something you can do to shift your existence to one with more power and fulfillment. It changes only by actively practicing the messages that will help you be your creative best. The practice doesn't need to be perfect, but it needs to be constant to change the automatic patterns you've created.

If you are not where you want to be creatively, be aware of what you are saying to yourself.

Experiment with what it would be like to tell yourself something different. Don't just practice the thoughts, practice how it would *feel* to believe them.

See the Self-Talk menu on pages 49-50.

HOW CHANGE REALLY SUCCEEDS

Pick one or use all three of the following:

ONE Give yourself permission to set a goal that's so easy your brain buys into it instead of rejects it. Instead of 100%, be 5% more trusting, deserving, or confident. Try it now.

TWO Try out a new way of being for an amount of time so short that it's easy to accept its feeling, then let go of the pressure to stay that way, rather than expectong yourself to sustain it from now on.

For just 15 SECONDS practice feeling more trusting, deserving, or successful.

THREE Use your imagination. Ask yourself, "What would it be like to trust the process?" For example: What if you pretended like you were one of those people who are audaciously creative? Ask What if . . . "What if I pretended I was an expert at what I do?" How would that feel?

IMAGINE

15 SECONDS

5%

THOUGHTS:

When the opportunity arises, I mess it up.
When things start going good, I also mess it up.
I disappoint people and myself.
I don't deserve good things.
It feels strangely weird when things are going well.

HERE ARE SOME THINGS YOU DO:

As you get close to success, you feel pressure and derail yourself by not following through or by burning a bridge.
You have abilities but you don't seem to let yourself use them.
You turn away or don't feel comfortable asking for help from others.
You set unrealistic expectations for yourself.
You disappoint people who could help you succeed by not showing up, being late, not doing what you said you'd do, ignoring them, and/or alienating them.

If you were exposed to a lot of disappointment when you were a child or often felt like nothing you did was ever enough, disappointment may be something that you do because it's in your programming. Your brain developed a propensity toward disappointment because, as it developed, disappointment was a regular element in your environment. If you begin to experience success or uncomfortable positive attention that feels foreign to you, subconsciously you may drift toward family loyalty and end up sabotaging yourself, thus creating the more familiar feeling of being disappointed.

Renowned Psychologist and Kaizen-Muse Creativity Coaching teacher, Robert Maurer provides these suggestions:
~Be aware of what's happening so the automatic nature of it can be stopped.
~Explore in a journal where you sabotaged yourself in the past, where you may continue to sabotage yourself. Where will you procrastinate instead of show up? Where might you disappoint someone or feel disappointed? When you find yourself doing what you've written, you are awake and can choose a different response. Know that this changes only over a period of repetitive practice.
~Begin to change your self-talk to accepting, encouraging, and compassionate versus harsh and disappointed.

ADDITIONAL SUGGESTIONS FROM THE MUSE:
~Give yourself permission not to disappoint yourself and those helping you. This could be as simple as announcing to yourself: "You have permission not to be sucked into the disappointment dynamic today." You take away the charge and the inner struggle by taking disappointment out of the picture.
~Practice relaxing with the feeling of success for just fifteen seconds at a time.
~Practice receiving help from others, even if it's a small percentage.
~Know that changing self-sabotage takes time and does not need to happen all at once. But if you keep returning to these tools, over time you will feel a shift that will change your life.
~Work with a gentle, compassionate creativity coach who understands that acceptance works better than intimidation, relentless pressure, and high expectations.

ISSUE:

PROCRASTINATION

THOUGHTS:
I keep putting off my creative time. Also, I never finish thin...

DESCRIPTION:
You are experiencing a flurry of rationalizations as to why it's okay to do something other than your Creative Adventure, often followed by self-flogging.

Procrastination, with all its decadent, underhanded, and irresistible machinations, has derailed your Willingness.

IF ALL THE UNFINISHED PROJECTS IN THE WORLD WERE PASTED TOGETHER, THEY WOULD MAKE ANOTHER WHOLE PLANET—BUT IT WOULD BE AN UNFINISHED PLANET. PROCRASTINATION IS COMMON.

BE UNCOMMON.

If you succumb to other activities because they are easier than the creative process, you might want to buck-up in the name of your purpose on the planet.

Consider showing up to your creative call in small increments of time over and over until you have created a new habit. The reward of self-respect will gradually inspire loyalty to creativity versus to sneaky rationalizations to the contrary.

Team up with a buddy and work at the same time even if it's in two different places for Parallel Universe Time. Call at the beginning and end of your time together. This is not only one of the most effective tools in beating procrastination, it also has a grounding, sacred feeling.

Shift your intent. Instead of showing up for your Creative Adventure to write a book, make a film, or develop a body of art, make it about self-love. Procrastination is a form of punishment. When you break through your procrastination, the esteem you gain becomes a strength you can use to be more confident in any endeavor in your life.

Shirley MacLaine once said: "I think of life itself now as a wonderful play that I've written for myself . . . and so my purpose is to have the utmost fun playing my part." Make your Creative Adventure a wonderful play you've written for yourself and your purpose is to have colossal fun playing your part. Close your eyes right now and imagine how that might look.

Make it a challenge: Dare yourself to go 20 minutes without a distraction and then give yourself 5 minutes of play as reward and start the challenge all over again.

Take a class. Make sure you find a teacher you relate to. Classes and workshops deepen your dedication and make it easy to show up.

If you can't show up for yourself, dedicate your time with your Creative Adventure to a precious person or a cause you believe in.

Dedicate 5 minutes at the beginning of the day to your Creative Adventure.

Here are some ways to use your dedicated five minutes of time:

~Take a moment and allow your intuition to decide what small step to take.

~Write one or two questions about your Creative Adventure and doodle, mind-map or list answers.

~Make a list of unfinished sentences about your Creative Adventure and play with finishing them.

~Set a date for your art show, a reading of your work, a deadline. Let it light a fire under your butt.

~Have a dress rehearsal for what you might do IF you were engaged in your Creative Adventure. The festive nature of this intention may keep the fear that causes procrastination at bay.

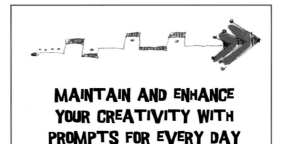

MAINTAIN AND ENHANCE
YOUR CREATIVITY WITH
PROMPTS FOR EVERY DAY
OF THE YEAR.

THE MORE YOU ENGAGE, THE
SMOOTHER AND MORE
BRILLIANT YOUR
CREATIVE ENGINES WILL
OPERATE.

I know you've heard it a thousand times before.
But it's true — hard work pays off. If you want
to be good, you have to practice, practice,
practice. If you don't love something, then don't
do it. ~Ray Bradbury

DAY-
TO-DAY
MAINTENANCE
DATEBOOK

THERE ARE AS MANY WORLDS AS THERE ARE
KINDS OF DAYS, AND AS AN OPAL CHANGES
ITS COLORS AND ITS FIRE TO MATCH THE
NATURE OF A DAY, SO DO I.
~JOHN STEINBECK

1 BEGIN AGAIN.

Remember what worked last year. Instigate passionate moments, one after another. Write three words that represent how you want to feel all year long. Write a journal entry as if it were December 31 and your year was AMAZING.

2 B-day of **LYNDA BARRY** who wrote in *What It Is*, "The thing I call 'my mind' seems to be kind of like a landlord that doesn't really know its tenants."
What kinds of tenants inhabit your mind? Who's in there? Judgment? An idea about your next collage? A title of a book? A thought that is in a constant loop? A love of beauty? A little kid? A meditating goddess? Make a list.

3 BACK TO THE TENANTS FROM YESTERDAY Do your tenants in your head complain about the noise, leave dirty laundry on the balcony, or hang strange black felt paintings on the wall? Pick one or two and have a dialogue? Make a visual journal page of a building with tenants that would represent the ones in your head. Or forget all that and review your three words from January 1.

4 Performance artist and actor, **LAURIE ANDERSON** said, "As an artist I'd choose the thing that's beautiful more than the one that's true." Artistic license often defies logic. Push yourself to complete this unfinished sentence at least five times: "As an artist (or writer)—"

5 B-day of **UMBERTO ECO,** who said, "The contents of someone's bookcase are part of his history, like an ancestral portrait." What's in your bookcase? Write about it as an observer, a historian, yourself, one of the books, OR As something other than a book that's on one of the shelves.

Tenants in your mind

6 B-day of **ROWAN ATKINSON**, who said, "We are as similar as two completely dissimilar peas in a pod." Embrace dissimilarnesses and contradictions. For practice at being novel, make a list of things you find to be dissimilar. Then pause and see if somehow loosely or metaphorically you find some similarities to those very same things. Or start a piece of writing with, "I am not at all similar to . . . "

JANUARY

7 e.e.cummings said, "Twice I've lived forever in a smile." Where have you lived "forever?" What sight or sensation touched you deeply enough to feel as if time stood still? Capture it forever in poetry, art, or music.

8 NICK BANTOCK said, "Art is like therapy; what comes up is what comes up. It may be dark, but that's what comes up. You may want to keep some of it in a drawer . . . but never judge it." Write or make art specifically for keeping it in a dark drawer underneath your long underwear. Listen to music that liberates emotion in your writing or art.

9 NEWSPAPER HEADLINE: "Steps being taken to keep fireflies from going out." Write a list of other fun headlines or of what it would take to keep *you* from "going out." Or review your three words from January 1.

10 Go back to the prompt on the 9th **ABOUT THE FIREFLIES** and pick one of the headlines on your list or one of the things that keep you lit, and write about it further, or use it as an inspiration for art or collage.

11 B-day of **ALAN PATON**, who said, "There is a hard law. When an injury is done to us, we never recover until we forgive. " Same goes for self-forgiveness. Explore it in writing, poetry, art, or movement to music in your living room.

12 B-day of author, **WALTER MOSELY**, who wrote, "The first thing you have to know about writing is that it is something you must do every day. There are two reasons for this rule: Getting the work done and connecting with your unconscious mind." Write today, even if it's just for 5 minutes. Begin with: "Hey, over here . . ."

13 B-day of short-story writer, **LORRIE MOORE** who wrote, "One should never turn one's back on a vivid imagination." What if a vivid imagination lived next store to you. What kind of things might be happening over there? Free-associate with a list or mind-map to personify a vivid imagination and explore one or more of you results in writing, art, playwrighting, or photography.

A Flock of Flaws

14 Ponder this quote from **PAUL VALLERY**:"Existence is no more than a flaw in the perfection of non-existence." Does that help you feel a little less worried about making mistakes? Try it out–write a poem about flaws, or paint them or make a mixed-media flock of them (like I did.)

15 B-day of **MARTIN LUTHER KING, JR.**, who said, "No person has the right to rain on your dreams." Celebrate your dreams today. Go do something dream-related.

16 B-day of writer **SUSAN SONTAG**. In her 1964 essay "Notes on Camp," Sontag suggested that even bad art could be appreciated, that there can be "a good taste of bad taste." The essay had a huge impact on the New York intellectual world, and Susan Sontag became a spokesperson for the American avant-garde. Use this as permission to make bad art, poetry, or prose just to see what happens. Free-associate to the word: Avant-garde

17 B-day of **WILLIAM STAFFORD,** who said, "Everyone is born a poet–a person discovering the way words sound and work, caring and delighting in words. I just kept on doing what everyone starts out doing. The real question is: Why did other people stop?"
If you delight in words, open a book, pull a bunch out and use them to write a quick poem. For extra credit, use the words you found, but begin with this sentence: "Everyone is born …"

18 B-day of author **A.A. MILNE** who said, "Ideas may drift into other minds, but they do not drift my way. I have to go and fetch them. I know no work manual or mental to equal the appalling heartbreaking anguish of fetching an idea from nowhere." Begin with one or more of these sentences, "Ideas are found…," or "Once I drifted into… " or "Out of nowhere . . ."

19 B-day of **EDGAR ALLAN POE** who said, "I was never really insane except upon occasions when my heart was touched." Have you ever felt your heart touched so much, you felt a little crazy? Write, scribble, dance about it. Do any dream-related thing today even if it's very small and keep the spirit of MLK's birthday going.

JANUARY

20 B-day of filmmaker **FEDERICO FELLINI**, who said, "All art is autobiographical. The pearl is the oyster's autobiography." What pearls can be strung together to make up your life? Draw a pearl necklace on a page, and without too much thought, write titles of little stories that make up your life. Let the stories be anything you think of from small lesser-known stories to profound life changing ones. Then listen to what your intuition wants to do with them next.

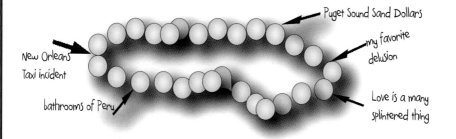

Puget Sound Sand Dollars

my favorite delusion

New Orleans Taxi incident

bathrooms of Peru

Love is a many splintered thing

21 RETURN TO YESTERDAY and pick a few of the stories and take them to the next step. In fact if there's any prompt you want to continue with, keep going with it–take it deep, practice it. If you're just reading these and not doing any of them, live on the edge. When the stubborn person inside of you is not looking, sneak writing or art for 3 minutes like a bandit. Steal your joy.

22 Write a list of at least 3 things you love about **YOUR CREATIVE PROCESS**. Breathe into these 3 things, and THEN, let them breathe into you. Make them big in your being. What if you acted as if a new idea is trying to find you? Write about it.

23 B-day of the painter **EDUOARD MANET**, who said, "There is only one true thing: instantly paint what you see. When you've got it, you've got it. When you haven't, you begin again. All the rest is humbug." Create a quick body of work focusing on one or two subjects: Doodle, collage, or paint a particular subject: apples, brooms, dancers, angels, dogs, cats, cactus blossoms, doors, windows, the view out of your window, banana cream pie. Just going for the experience without worrying about quality. Render multiple versions of the same subject.

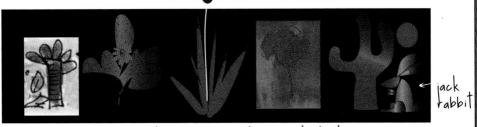

jack rabbit

quick body of work: desert plants

24 B-day of journal writer and novelist, **EDITH WHARTON**. Imagine you were having a conversation with Edith, she said one of the quotes below. Write what you would say back.

"Ah, good conversation–there's nothing like it, is there? The air of ideas is the only air worth breathing."

"Life is always either a tightrope or a feather bed. Give me the tightrope."

"Nothing is more perplexing to a man than the mental process of a woman who reasons her emotions."

"Creativity is a continual surprise." –Ray Bradbury

25 Use the **ALPHABET** as your structure to write a list of up to 26 random words that you find interesting or different. Pick one or more of those words and write or create art around it. Or use several of them, adding more as needed for poetry or prose. For example: A–albino, B–bathtub C–curved, D–delivery, E–electric F–foofaraw.
(Warning: Never use an electric foofaraw in the bathtub.)

26 If you drove **A BUMPER CAR**, (free of the guide-rails), where would you go, who would you bump into, and why?
Write about it using haiku, just five lines, or narrate yourself in motion.

27 B-day of **LEWIS CARROLL**, who said, "Begin at the beginning and go on till you come to the end; then stop." Write a list of similarly obvious directions, or take Carroll's version and make variations on it. Creative exercises like this expand your imagination so that more ideas are readily accessible when you engage in other endeavors.

28 B-day of **COLETTE**, who said, "Time spent with a cat is never wasted." Raise your hand if you agree.

If you didn't raise your hand, what would you replace with the word, "cat"? Write, sketch, doodle, haiku, make a tuna-sculpture tribute to a cat or your cat-replacement.

29 If there were a **RAPID TIME-LAPSE FILM** of how we spent our lives, we would see ourselves doing and thinking the same things over and over. While doing one of your repeat actions today, imagine yourself in a film or documentary and do something different just for the creative sensation. Write about it. Considering adding a sound track.

30 B-day of **RICHARD BRAUTIGAN**, who said, "I have always wanted to write a book that ended with the word mayonnaise." And he did. Write a poem or piece ending with "mayonnaise." If you like that challenge, try ending with one of these words: once, alone, mountains, live, bounce.

31 B-day of **THOMAS MERTON**, who said, "Hurry ruins saints as well as artists." Perspective: Go slow. Take your Creative Adventure and savor, consider, pause, reflect, nurture, and hold sacred. Try moving in slow motion while you work on it and notice how much more present you are. Then try the opposite—go fast. See which one works for you in the moment. There's merit to both.

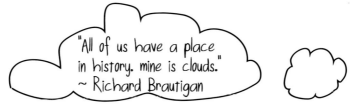

"All of us have a place in history. mine is clouds."
~ Richard Brautigan

SOMETIMES AN ARTIST'S
FIRST INVENTION IS HERSELF.
~STEPHANIE VAUGHN

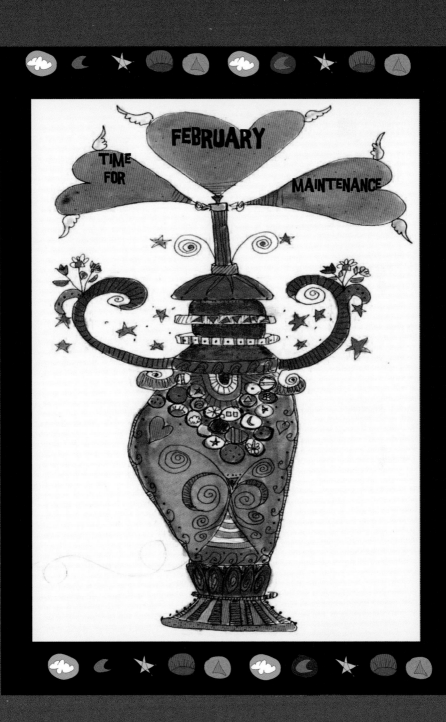

FEBRUARY

1 Artist **MARCEL DUCHAMP** said, "I force myself to contradict myself in order to avoid conforming to my own taste." What contradiction would help your current creative focus? Write about or create something that contradicts what you might normally do in any area of your creativity.

2 B-day of **JAMES JOYCE**, who is best known for *Ulysses*, the novel that perfected his stream of consciousness technique, which, as you may know, is the written equivalent of someone's thought process and can make associative leaps like a frog leaping from a lily pad to a beer commercial, a continuous flow of sense-perceptions, thoughts, feelings, and memories in the human mind not paying particular attention to punctuation, which if you say punctuation with enunciated punch, is sort of an onomatopoeia which could also be mistaken for a main course in a Greek restaurant . . . ouzo! Write your own stream of consciousness thought with associative leaps. For extra credit, begin with: "I took a leap into . . ." or "I'd like to punch . . ."

3 B-day of philosopher **SIMONE WEIL**, who said, "Absolutely unmixed attention is prayer."
Performance artist Laurie Anderson said, "Art is about paying attention." Experiment with finding a different level of attention for yourself. Give yourself a 15-minute field trip called "Mission Attention." Ask yourself "What out there is waiting to inspire an idea inside of me?" Multitasking can rob us of the moment's possibility.

4 B-day of author **STEWART O'NAN**, who encourages people who want to be writers to carry around a notebook: "If you don't write it down, it's gone." Whether you are an artist, a writer, or someone who likes to remember ideas and funny things, do you have a little notebook within which to capture inspiration and doodles? Take a walk with a notebook and notice that it actually encourages the discovery of ideas. If this doesn't work for you, act like it does. Put a metallic stick on the front of your notebook and pretend it's an idea magnet for your notebook.

I want to write a book about shoes that's full of footnotes. ~Jarod Kintz

5 Actor and comedian, **CHRISTOPHER GUEST** said, "I don't work with high-concept things that start with a premise, [like] 'Wouldn't it be funny if there was this spy who met a...' For me, it could be, 'What about people who sell shoes? That must be a bizarre world... when they meet at conventions and talk about shoes.'" Create poetry, art, or story about shoes: your favorite pair, a shoe-related incident, or shoes that talk to you.

6 B-day of food writer **MICHAEL POLLAN**. In one of his books he wrote, "He showed the words 'chocolate cake' to a group of Americans and recorded their word associations. 'Guilt' was the top response. If that strikes you as unexceptional, consider the response of French eaters to the same prompt: 'celebration.'" Write a list of associations you have and ones you'd like to have to the following words: chocolate, relax, trust, art, carefree, satisfied, work, age, live, mortality, relationship.

7 B-day of author **SINCLAIR LEWIS**, who said, "It is impossible to discourage the real writers–they don't give a damn what you say, they're going to write." Percolator: What if you acted as if you were a real writer or artist (If you don't already)? How would "not giving a damn" feel? Practice feeling this way just 5% more. Can you let yourself create writing or art just because you want to and for no other reason? Write a short, embellished bio about yourself as a writer or artist.

FEBRUARY

8 B-day of **JULES VERNE**, who said, "I believe cats to be spirits come to earth. A cat, I am sure, could walk on a cloud without coming through." Suspend logic: Write a list of imaginary beliefs starting with, "I believe . . ." Doodle, depict, or write a poem either about cats (or dogs, hamsters, birds) on clouds or write about anything from your list of imaginary beliefs.

Paw-don Me

9 B-day of **ALICE WALKER**, who said, "The most common way people give up their power is by thinking they don't have any." Power up. Write about yourself in the second person as if you believed in your power. What does the feeling of more confidence feel like in her body? What would he do differently today if he felt 5% more creatively powerful? Act as if you have power; start by thinking powerful thoughts. Try one now but don't scare the cat.

10 Find ten words in a book or magazine and use them as **RAW MATERIALS** for a poetry, prose, or mixed media art piece. Add more words as needed. Be strangely impressed with yourself. Extra credit: Begin with this unfinished sentence: "I'm strangely impressed with myself… "

11 B-day of **THOMAS EDISON**, who said, "If we all did the things we are capable of, we would astound ourselves." Write down what you've done this week and summon up astonishment. To practice original thinking, act astonished about something mundane, like how both feet don't try to walk at the same time, how your eyes blink without your thinking about it, and the color blue.

*"To be astonished is one of the surest ways of not growing old too quickly."
~Colette*

12 B-day of **CHARLES DARWIN,** who said, "If I had my life to live over again, I would have made a rule to read some poetry and listen to some music at least once a week." Put this book down, go read some poetry or listen to music with undivided attention. Even if it's for just 5 minutes. Or write 3 haikus about the weather, birds, or impending Valentine's Day.

13 B-day of witty writer **MARGARET HALSEY,** who said, "Humility is not my forte, and whenever I dwell for any length of time on my own shortcomings, they gradually begin to seem mild, harmless, rather engaging little things, not at all like the staring defects in other people's characters." Pick one of your shortcomings and write an endearing haiku, poem, or essay about it as if it were something sweet.

*So I park crooked.
It's only because I have
Artistic License.*

14 **Valentine's Day**. Scavenger hunt for Raw Materials:
List a street name, a fruit, a color, some part of nature, something in your closet, an adjective, to describe the sky, and then use these words (add more as you need them) in a love poem, even if their meaning is different from the original context. If you don't have a "valentine" today, create "havoc" by writing an acronym for HAVOC. Or send love to a bunch of your friends and one person who completely doesn't expect something from you or someone with whom you fell out of touch.

15 B-day of *The Simpsons'* creator **MATT GROENING**, who said, "Well, most grown-ups forget what it was like to be a kid. I vowed that I would never forget." Remember something today that you loved about being a kid, and do or create something that represents it; for example, make paper dolls. Or treat yourself to a festive outing and some vanilla pudding.

16 What about the word, "**MIDDLE**"? What does "the middle" mean to you? Write about the middle. What are you in the middle of right now?

*I'm in the middle
of writing a short haiku,
Wait! haikus ARE short.*

FEBRUARY

17 B-day of writer **RUTH RENDELL**, who wrote in *One Across, Two Down*, "We always know when we are awake that we cannot be dreaming even though when actually dreaming we feel all this may be real."

Exercise your muscles of imaginary thinking by imagining that what you are experiencing right now is a dream with which you can awaken. Feel surrealistic. What would you awaken to? What about this dream do you like best? Begin writing, "This dream . . ."

18 B-day of **TONI MORRISON**, who wrote in *Beloved*, "Sweet, crazy conversations full of half sentences, daydreams and misunderstandings more thrilling than understanding could ever be." Make a list of sweet, crazy, half sentences, daydreams and misunderstandings and then weave them into poetry or prose.

MORTALS MUST DO WHAT THEY ARE HERE TO DO CREATIVELY OR THEY WILL BECOME CRANKY.

19 B-day of **KAY BOYLE**, who said, "There is only one history of any importance, and it is the history of what you once believed in, and the history of what you came to believe in." Keep going, finding different completions: "I once believed …" or "I came to believe …, now I believe . . ."

20 In her book, *Grapefruit*, **YOKO ONO** wrote quirky, off-the-wall directions like, "Count all the words in a book instead of reading them," and "Put one memory in one half of your head. Shut it off and forget it. Let the other half of your brain long for it."

Make up some of your own random directions. Here's one of mine:

Place your feet pigeon-toed.
Stare at the sky.
If you see a pigeon . . . wave.

21 B-day of **JONATHAN SAFRAN FOER**, who wrote in *Extremely Loud and Incredibly Close*, "I spent my life learning to feel less. Every day I felt less. Is that growing old? Or is it something worse?" and, "You cannot protect yourself from sadness without protecting yourself from happiness."

Pick one or both of these quotes and reflect about protecting yourself from your feelings or write about how you allow yourself to be open to the gamut of pain and joy.

Or just pick two opposing feelings and give them freedom to express themselves how they want.

22 B-day of comedienne **RACHEL DRATCH**. Tina Fey is quoted as saying, "I regularly ate health food cookies so disgusting that when I enthusiastically gave one to Rachel Dratch, she drew a picture of a rabbit and broke the cookie into a trail of tiny pieces coming out of the rabbit's butt." Sometimes creativity can be pretty silly. Mind-map the word "silly."
Write something about your butt, butts in general, or your feelings about health food cookies. You don't need to be funny, just explore a conversation.

23 Take a walk outside, observe your surroundings, but strip them of their labels. Instead of seeing grass, trees, houses, etc, see their shapes, lines, colors, shades and sizes without the names. Take a note pad and write any phrases or feelings other than labels that come to you. Or take photos.

gravelly
rectangular
oval

24 B-day of **STEVE JOBS**, who said, "It's more fun to be a pirate than to join the army." How can you be a pirate today? How can you sail your own ship rather than follow a fleet that all looks the same? In a visual journal, create your own ship and/or write about your uniqueness, beginning with, "I'm different because . . ."

25 With the swiftness of a writer on caffeine, write down **25 RANDOM MEMORIES** in any order: big ones, small ones, warped and sacred ones.
Memories are filled with creative potential and are usually embellished with conscious and subconscious interpretations. Choose a memory, give it a title, and reconstruct it as prose in third person, poetry, a news report, a visual journaling page. As you do this, you may notice more memories begin arriving. Have a list to which you can add them. Consider reinterpreting negative memories from a different point of view—could be life-changing. Or not.

February

26 B-day of **VICTOR HUGO**, who said, "Laughter is the sun that drives winter from the human face." Make a list of your favorite sources of laughter. See if you can remember any recent laughs; we are the only animal that can relive laughter over and over (I think). Write a poem or haiku, make art from laughter's point of view.
Begin a piece with, "I laugh when . . . "

27 Walking can exercise not only your leg muscles but **YOUR CREATIVITY MUSCLES** as well. If you alternate looking right and then left as you walk, you are stimulating brain pathways. Take a walk and look from side to side and linger on what you see for just a few seconds. Let your eyes quickly take snapshots of objects and shapes. Imagine that you are walking through an exhibit of objects with no names. You'll realize the world is filled with art. Write about your findings. Consider returning to an object with a camera to capture and write about an observation. Extra credit: Collect found objects, assemble, and photograph in various designs.

28 **JOURNAL WRITING** enhances the creative process in myriad ways. Make it a treat, a time you get to talk to yourself about ideas, savor moments, and play with Thinking Caps to see your life from different perspectives. Show up for it the same time every day even if it's just 5 minutes; if it's a habit, it's easier.

29 My first **ART TRAINING** came from my grandma, who, one morning over Welch's grape juice, taught me to draw animals like the ones you see below. I was hooked. The rest of my training came from doodling in Algebra class to allay the anxiety of trying to decipher left-brain gibberish. An obsession with doodling was responsible for the rest. Formal education is not required for creativity. Practice and passion are. Practice a passion today; begin by simply thinking about it. Consider doodling.

LIFE BEATS DOWN AND CRUSHES
THE SOUL AND ART REMINDS
YOU THAT YOU HAVE ONE.
~STELLA ADLER

MARCH
MAINTENANCE

MARCH

1 B-day of actor, film director, screenwriter, and producer **ZACK SNYDER**, who wrote in *Sucker Punch*: "Everyone has an angel. A guardian who watches over us. We can't know what form they'll take. One day old man, next day little girl . . . Yet they are not here to fight our battles, but to whisper from a hearth. Reminding that it's us . . . it's everyone of us who holds the power of the worlds we create."
Let your guardian have a conversation on the page with you using prose or poetry to convey some wisdom. Depict guardians of all different shapes, sizes, and species in a visual journal and notice how their power is more present when you do.

2 B-day of **DR. SEUSS** (Theodore Geisel), who said, "I like nonsense, it wakes up the brain cells. Fantasy is a necessary ingredient in living." Make a list of nonsense sentences that simply make you smile. Consider illustrating one or two with collage or doodles.

3 Author and travel writer **PICO IYER** said, "The less conscious one is of being 'a writer,' the better the writing." Take 5 minutes to write as if you were just having a conversation with a friend who is easy to talk to. Or write to the same friend about your Creative Adventure, hobbies you used to have, a hobby you'll have when you're 80, or where you were last night.

4 Artist **ISAAC JULIEN** says, "I'm always on the lookout–I observe people in the street, I watch films, I read, I think about the conversations that I have. It's about taking all the little everyday things and observing them with a critical eye; building up a scrapbook which you can draw on. Sometimes, too, I look at other artworks or films to get an idea of what not to do." Go into observation mode for a few days and add observations to an on-going scrapbook.

133

5 Poet **GEORGE SANTAYANA** said, "Art is delayed echo."
Repeat and complete over and over: "**ART IS** ..."
For instance:
Art is witness.
Art is a frozen moment.
Art is letting go.
Go fast, don't worry about making sense, or repeating. Just go.
Then, without getting up, to check the fridge, your cell phone or
the Internet, continue by repeating and completing: **I AM** ...
"Art is witness and I am guilty with breaking and entering bliss."

6 Architect **SUNAND PRASAD** advises that for inspiration keep asking: "What is going on here?" He says ask offbeat questions like, "What if this library were a garden?" or "If this facade could speak, would it be cooing, swearing, silent, or erudite?"
Quickly make a list of similar questions. Add to it often.

7 Return to your list of questions from yesterday and write answers. Suggested approach: Take the question **"WHAT IF THIS LIBRARY WERE A GARDEN?"** and change it to "If this library were a garden it ..." and keep going.
And/or write a poem or haiku about the bird to the right, there, with the coffee pot on his head.

8 WORD POOL Use some or all of the following words or phrases in poetry, prose, art, mumbling, ranting, cooing, etc., and add words as you need them. If only one of the words takes you on a journey, go with it: Choose from these words: bend, right, under, crayon, in a way, avenue, keys, have, blunder, bare, forest, infinite, answers, fiddle, gently, garage, putter.

MARCH

9 For a creative exercise that's mischievous, visually interesting, and/or an outlet for venting psychological debri **CUT THE HEADS** off of images and replace them with other more artistic heads. For a further adventure: Write about it. Or write about the trio below. Where are they going? What happens next? What's the dialogue?

10 Let **AN EMPTY GLASS** inspire poetry, art, photography, or a smoothie. Use it as a lens, turn it upside down over something.

11 B-day of creative genius musician **BOBBY MCFERRIN**, who said, "I like to use the audience as my color palette, my instrument." Write a list of people in your life. Use them as a palette or instrument and assign colors, emotions, and random words to each of them. Now paint, write, or collage from that multimedia palette. Or just love them.

12 B-day of **JACK KEROUAC**, whose first rule in his *Belief and Technique for Modern Prose* is, "1. Scribbled secret notebooks, and wild typewritten pages, for yr own joy wrote." Giving no thought to whether it's any good, scribble secrets, real or fictional, in an upside-down notebook or get on the computer like a wild, crazed beatnik. (curse the establishment out loud), and write edgy poetry even if you think you don't know how.

Live, travel, adventure, bless, and don't be sorry. ~Jack Kerouac

13 Use the **ALPHABET** as a warm-up. This time go from A to M listing experiences, feelings and thoughts you've had in the past week. (For example A: Apples, found two huge delicious ones at the Farmers Market on Sunday; B: Butt fell asleep today while writing the book; C: Craved Chocolate, went to See's outlet center yesterday(free samples: dark chocolate-covered almonds); D: Deciding things (personal–none of your business); E: Etc. If any of these topics are asking to be more, like a poem, art, an essay, prose–comply.

14 Do **N-Z** of the Alphabet (see yesterday's instructions or break the rules and do your own thing, like just use T).

15 *Inner Game of Golf* author, **TIM GALLWEY** said, "Relaxed concentration is the key to excellence in all things." With relaxed concentration, write a list of things you think might be more excellent if they were done with … relaxed concentration. Seriously. Try going through your day with a soft focus vision and notice how it keeps you in the present moment.

16 Practice **RELAXED CONCENTRATION** with one of the items you listed yesterday. Work in slow motion and notice how that keeps you present too. Putting your eyes into a soft focus also keeps you present.

17 ST. PATRICK'S DAY. Mind map: Write a diary entry from the point of view of **THE COLOR GREEN**. For extra credit, include one or all of the following words and phrases: make-believe, not sure what that was, luck, and wind.

18 B-day of **JOHN UPDIKE**, who said, "I can't bear to finish things, beyond a certain point they get heavy. There's something so dead about a finished painting." Purposely write or create something and stop before you think it is finished and allow it to still be alive. If you're stuck for subjects, let the theme be: The backyard. See what happens.

NOTE TO SELF: Let the world be in soft focus today.

19 OBSESS about your Creative Adventure, as if it were your lover. Think about it ALL the time. Write it a love letter, let it write you one back. Think of all the ways you can woo your creativity by mind-mapping or writing a list starting with the trigger:"I could . . ." and rapidly filling it in, speeding past the limits of the mind.

20 B-day of **HENRIK IBSEN**, who wrote a play ending with a wife leaving her husband and slamming the door. It was so shocking to nineteenth-century viewers that it was known as "the door slam heard around the world." Write, create art, photography, or a dance about a door slamming.

21 SPRING EQUINOX Invent a new Spring Ritual. Consider including cupcakes, fruit, or hats with flowers in them.
Or find a painting and make a flower arrangment that florally depicts or complements the image.

22 USE THE WORD "**FORAGE.**" Interpret intuitively. Make a list of ways to forage, make an acronym or acrostic.

23 B-day of writer and humorist **JACKIE BOUCHARD,** who said, "You're relying on your thesaurus too much when you tell that special someone he makes you feel tepid and hirsute inside." (Synonyms for warm and fuzzy.) Play with the thesaurus. Take some common phrases and/or cliches and see what funny or different words can replace them.

24 B-day of poet **LAWRENCE FERLINGHETTI**, who said, "Poetry is the shadow cast by our streetlight imaginations." Here are some words and phrases from Ferlinghetti poems. Assemble and add more words for your own piece; feel free to split phrases up: streetlight, risking absurdity, other side of the day, empty air, a breathless hush, grand boulevard with trees, wilderness, we think differently at night.

25 FLANNERY O'CONNOR'S

B-day. She said, "The writer should never be ashamed of staring. There is nothing that does not require his attention." Stare at something today and ask, "Where might this take me creatively?" "What is this all about?" Or just stare and let what you're staring at ask questions of you.

26 B-day of JOSEPH CAMPBELL,

who wrote, "If the path before you is clear, you're probably on someone else's." What's on your path, metaphorically and literally? Write a description about what's on a path you're taking. What evidence of greatness is on your path? Where is your bliss leading you?

27 B-day of filmmaker QUENTIN TARANTINO,

who said, "I was kind of excited to go to jail for the first time and I learnt some great dialogue." What locations previously considered undesirable can be good resources for good dialog? Make a list of places. Make a list of dialog you might hear from those places.

28 B-day of VIRGINIA WOOLF,

who wrote, "The eyes of others our prisons; their thoughts our cages." List the ways you may be influenced by the opinions of others. Write about opening the cage and audaciously reentering the world with unfettered loyalty to your creative self, because, you know what? It's also the B-day of **LADY GAGA**, who reinforces this theme by saying, "Don't you ever let a soul in the world tell you that you can't be exactly who you are."

29 B-day of author and comedienne, AMY SEDARIS.

In her book, *I Like You: Hospitality Under the Influence,* she writes about who to invite to your party: "Guest Lists: If everyone is the same, the party is a boring convention. Still, you should avoid toxic combinations, like an astrologer and an astronomer, the newly divorced couple, and a serial killer and a drunken teenager." Pick one of those couples or another unlikely combination and write a dialog between them, or in the case of the killer and the teenager, a dark poem.

30 Rewrite, revisit, restore, renew, reiterate, re-MIND, **RECESS!!** (Really.)

MARCH 31

didn't fit
on the last
page so it
has a whole page
of its own.

Your **CREATIVE ENGINES** operate most efficiently when your mind, body, and emotions feel energetic and taken care of.

Exercise, diet, attitude all affect energy.

Do a Quick Systems Check on These Areas:

☐ Am I eating in a way that optimizes my energy?

☐ How's it feel creatively when I take a walk or get good aerobic activity?

☐ Do I need to do something with all this stress in my life like talk about it, meditate, journal, or exercise vigorously--even if it's just in the interest of feeling more energetically creative?

Physical fitness is not only one of the most important keys to a healthy body, it is the basis of dynamic and creative intellectual activity.
—John F. Kennedy

Hiya! Just hanging by the cupcake *stand in case you need me. I just eat these on special occasions. Luckily I'm creative so I'm always inventing special occasions.

CUPcakes

*I also eat mangoes when sugar makes me weird.

EVERYTHING IN LIFE IS ART.
FROM HOW YOU WALK AND
HOW YOU SMILE AT A
STRANGER, TO HOW YOU LOVE
SOMEONE AND THE WAY YOU
CHOOSE TO FEEL. IT'S ART.

APRIL
MAINTENANCE

APRIL

1 Create acronyms for the word **FOOLISH**. For instance: "**F**red **O**ffered **O**lives **L**ike **I**t's **S**omething **H**eavenly. "What comes to mind when you hear the words "fool" or "fooled"? Write a foolish haiku.

2 B-day of **HANS CHRISTIAN ANDERSEN**, who said, "Where words fail, music speaks." Put some music on and let it inspire writing, art, doodling, or simply a different perspective. Or simply listen to music. Revise this quote with your own sentence completion/s:
"Where words fail . . . "

3 Write three **SENSATIONS** you enjoyed in the last few days (tastes, smells, tactile, sight), then write details about those sensations. Next do something unexpected with what you wrote.

4 B-day of **MAYA ANGELOU**, who wrote, "Everything has rhythm, everything dances." Make a list of everything around you that has rhythm and dances. Consider using the Creativity Tool of Being Absurd while you list. Then make what you listed into a poem or visual journaling page.

5 Think of **ALL THE PLACES YOU'VE LIVED**, choose one, and let it write about you. Let it give its opinion about who you were living with, how it ended, how you decorated what you spent your time doing, and your quirks and habits.

6 **KEEP GOING** with one or more of these incomplete sentences:
"If I am out of my mind . . ."
"When the front door opened . . ."
"We danced . . ."
"The duck gazed out the window . . ."

7 B-day of **WILLIAM WORDSWORTH**, who said,
"Delight and liberty, the simple creed of childhood."
Write a simple creed for your kid-like self to follow in the creative process. Complete the sentence: "To be creative . . ." several times as if you were the creative kid inside of you or forget this, and let your kid-self make up the rules.

Make a wish.

STILL APRIL

8 B-day of author **BARBARA KINGSOLVER**. Reply to her quote as if you were having a conversation with her:

"The very least you can do in your life is figure out what you hope for. And the most you can do is live inside that hope. Not admire it from a distance, but live right in it, under its roof."

9 B-day of poet, **CHARLES BAUDELAIRE**, who said, "If the word doesn't exist, invent it; but first be sure it doesn't exist." Invent three words and incorporate them into a poem, prose, scutterhellmud, conversation with someone you want to confuse, or a visual journaling page.

10 B-day of author **ANNE LAMOTT**, who said:
"If there is one door in the castle you have been told not to go through, you must. Otherwise, you'll just be rearranging furniture in rooms you've already been in."
Percolators: What door have you been told not to go through?
What are you not supposed to write or depict visually?
Keep going: "So I opened the door and went in . . . "

11 Trigger word: **WANDER.** Free associate or mind-map the word. Combine two or more associations or pick one and write about it. Or let a doodle wander all over a page then put a watercolor wash on top.

12 Write a **DESCRIPTION** of your Creative Adventure as if you were a writer for a magazine describing the work of a famous artist, writer, person who lives artistically.
Or write a poem about a meal you had.

13 Here's a list of **TIM JANIS** songs: *Surrounding Wonder, Floating Moon, Beyond, , Where Dreams Begin, Here and Ever After.* Pick one and use it as a title, or combine them as Raw Materials for poetry, prose, collage, doodles, an abstract, dialogue in a play, or a conversation with your beloved.

14 What element of **NATURE** best represents you as an artist, writer, or person? Have it write about itself in first person, show up in an approach to your work, or take you on a journey.

15 **IMAGINE** and, if you're ambitious, depict any resistance you have to your creativity as if it were a large artistic sculpture.
What would it look like?
Now imagine and, if you like, artistically depict a door, that once you walk through it, takes you to the other side of your resistance.
What does it look like over there?
Conjure up these images each time you need to get through your resistance.

16 B-day of **KINGSLEY AMIS**, who wrote,
"Consciousness was upon him before he could get out of the way." Continue with his sentence in stream of consciousness writing, but change it to first person like this:
"Consciousness was upon me before I could get out of the way . . ."
Or write about being unconscious starting with: "So, this is unconsciousness, not what I expected . . ."

17 Speaking of **CONSCIOUSNESS**, it's the B-day of playwright Thornton Wilder, who said, "We can only be said to be alive in those moments when our hearts are conscious of our treasures." What would you consider your top ten treasures in this moment? Take a moment to imagine, list, and consider what your top ten treasures might be ten years from now. Celebrate with poetry, prose, or art.

Note to Self: If someone catches you going through the doors in the castle you weren't supposed to go through, just smile and act like you were supposed to be there.

18 Use your **CLOTHES** as inspiration for art or writing. What stories or inspiration for art are hidden in the fabric, facings, and pockets of your clothes? Seams like you could discover a lot to hem and ha about.

19 If you could be a part of **NATURE'S MAJESTY,** what would you be: A sunrise? A waterfall? A volcano? Write from its point of view, only revealing what it is, by what it's saying.

20 Use the **ALPHABET** as a starter. For each letter, A-M, come up with a word for something in your past for which you are grateful. If you have time, go for N-Z, things you have to look forward to. If you don't like those ideas, use the Alphabet to brainstorm ideas for the next step of your Creative Adventure, (e.g. A= ask questions, B= bathe while daydreaming, C= collect images and combine them, D=dust off an old journal and see if there's a poem worth revising, E=Etc.).

21 B-day of naturalist, **JOHN MUIR**, who said, "The clearest way into the Universe is through a forest wilderness." Find some nature, cease multitasking, and look and listen for what you might have formerly missed. Find the universe in a forest, on a beach, in your garden or in a simple leaf, bloom, or breeze. Begin a piece of writing or a visual journaling page with: "In this universe . . .

22 B-day of painter **RICHARD DIEBENKORN,** who said, "I don't go into the studio with the idea of 'saying' something. What I do is face the blank canvas and put a few arbitrary marks on it that start me on some sort of dialogue."
What few arbitrary words can you put on the page to start you on some sort of dialogue? Do this with writing or try it with doodling.

23 Write an acronym or acrostic for the word: **SENTENCE.**

24 George W. Curtis said, "Imagination is as good as many voyages—and how much cheaper." Take a voyage into your **IMAGINATION**. What will you pack? What will you wear? Where will you go if you could go anywhere? What stores would there be? What scenic bypasses? Who would you meet? Create and describe some photographs about the journey. Make a list under this topic: "Things I did on My Journey to THERE."

25 B-day of philosopher **LUDWIG WITTGENSTEIN**, who said, "Suppose someone were to say, 'Imagine this butterfly exactly as it is, but ugly instead of beautiful.'" Explore your mental malleability. Look at something you find ugly, and imagine it as beautiful. Imagine something mundane as extraordinary. Write or visually journal using this concept as inspiration. If you don't like this creative act, imagine that you LOVE it. See what happens.

26 B-day of novelist **BERNARD MALAMUD**, who said "Revision is one of the exquisite pleasures of writing." There is a certain pleasure and even therapy in sculpting sentences by eliminating words or replacing some of them with better contenders. Do some revising. Take a piece of writing and edit it poetically. Cut words out, put the middle at the beginning, change the point of view from first to third or third to first, embellish with exaggeration. Or write about shooting stars.

Imaginary journey, here we come.

27 Terri Guillemets wrote, "If you've never been thrilled to the very edges of your soul by **A FLOWER IN SPRING BLOOM**, maybe your soul has never been in bloom."

Find or buy a flower and contemplate it in slow-motion for at least 3 minutes, which doesn't seem like a long time, but with our shortened attention spans you'd be surprised–invent what a slow motion contemplation is. Set a timer. Zone in on any detail and make it the focus. Can you really see it? Experience it? Write to it, or have it write to you. Invent a world around it. Repeat with a different flower. Or make a mindmap or a bouquet of doodles around the theme, "Bloom."

28 B-day of author **TERRY PRATCHETT**, who said, "Fantasy is an exercise bicycle for the mind. It might not take you anywhere, but it tones up the muscles that can. Of course, I could be wrong."

He was right. Write or visually journal about yourself in the realm of fantasy. What would be the first line of your fantasy novel if you wrote one? Extra credit: Include the words: fire, bridge, wings, and window.

29 RANDY THOM said, "Nothing paralyzes an artist more than fear of screwing up. The first step toward curing writer's block is to begin writing, even if the most you can manage is to type random words. Writer's block is not the inability to type. It is the inability to type something of value. So you begin to cure it by typing anything." Open a book and just start copying what you see until you start writing on your own.

30 Andrea Owen wrote, "**IMPERFECT** is the new sexy." How can you embrace that today or during the next move in your Creative Journey?

Use the following word pool, adding the following words as you need them, to write an imperfect prose or poetry piece, or to inspire a less-than-perfect visual journal entry:

vase, sunrise, inexplicable, mix, sudden, stumble, elm, single, pot, arrange, wink, messenger, rise, angle of light.

YOU CAN'T BE THAT KID
STANDING AT THE TOP OF
THE WATERSLIDE,
OVERTHINKING IT.
YOU HAVE TO GO DOWN THE
CHUTE. ~TINA FEY

MAY-
TENANCE

MAY

1 This is the day celebrated as the arrival of Spring, contrary to the fact that it actually starts in March. So in the same spirit, let's also make this **YOUR OTHER BIRTHDAY.** Write about how this day could be celebrated differently. (If it's already your birthday, do this on Sept. 1.) Keep going with: It's just that I am . . .

2 B-day of writer and humorist **JEROME K. JEROME**, who said, "I like work: it fascinates me. I can sit and look at it for hours." Removing the pressure and just looking at your work with no expectations, can result in some interesting responses. Try it and then write about it, or not. Or stare at your hand, then write about it, or draw it with your nondominant hand.

3 Create a **BLURB** about yourself as if you are a famous person who is quoted, and then feel as if you are. You have permission to write a mundane or a magical quote. For example: Jill Badonsky was quoted as saying, "Lunch is best when eaten at 12:30, but chocolate can be eaten anytime."

4 Write **FOUR** things you would like to be thankful for six months from now. Write four things you're glad you did this week. Write four titles of works you would like to write about or create.

5 B-day of **JAMES BEARD**. In 1946, he launched the world's first cooking show, called, *I Love To Eat.* Write a list of what you love to eat and write a quick scene of how you might present these things in a cooking show or in a cooking article. Use Thinking Caps to come from a different point of view than you normally would. For instance, be mischeivous, sloppy, anal, angry, or paranoid as a cooking show host. Devote a visual journaling page to cooking, even if it's metaphorical cooking.

6 Keep going or repeat and complete differently at least six times: "The day is **VIBRATING** with . . . " (Feel free to add something absurd).

7 Artist-writer, Robert Genn said, "In art, everyone who plays **WINS**. "Visualize the next step of your Creative Adventure, see yourself playful in the process. What happens next? How did you win? Or write about the legs of chairs, a flock of herons, or your cousin.

8 Modify the meaning of R.I.P. Let it be a wake-up call every time you see it. Perhaps is stands for: **RAUCOUSLY INSTIGATE PASSION**. Here's a definiton from Lynda Treger, a member in my Writing Club: "Frozen in time, she realized it was probably too late to rest in peace, for there were still dreams to be conquered, dance steps to learn, kisses to give . . . used up habits to dump. I want to die while on my own dirt road, not in the passing lane of others. She 'Romanced Inner Passions' is what I want my goodbyes to whisper."

9 Here's how I sometimes like to write in my **JOURNAL**: "It was in that moment when she looked through the window and noticed the morning glories were applauding and the hummingbirds laughing, that she knew for sure the world was extraordinary (though somewhat esoteric)." Using that entry and Lynda Treger's quote above as examples, write dreamy things about your world in the third person.

10 B-day of author and philosopher **JEAN HOUSTON**, who wrote, "Our senses are indeed our doors and windows on this world, in a very real sense the key to the unlocking of meaning and the wellspring of creativity."
Write across the top of a page: Touch, See, Smell, Taste, Hear and then free-associate a list underneath. Take one of your responses and mind-map it, and then corral the words from the mind map into poetry, prose, or an entry in a visual journal.

11 B-day of writer **JEREMIAH ION**, who said: "Creativity . . . requires that you pay attention to it, and I have tried my best to take heed of its call. To let creativity truly run free in your life is to find happiness in all things." Take that last line into the depth of your soul, let it be your mantra, your guide, and put it on your to-do list.

To let creativity
truly run free
in your life
is to find happiness
in all things.

MAY

Cloud 8

"Cloud nine gets all the publicity, but cloud eight actually is cheaper, less crowded, and has a better view."
~George Carlin

12 B-day of comedian **GEORGE CARLIN**, who said, "Think off-center." Write words in a circle in the middle of a page. Suggestions: Titles for poetry or art, plans this summer, first lines, the next step of your Creative Adventure. Now make bubbles off to the side, and allow your fluid stream of ideas in those bubbles to be a little off-center, quirky, or absurd.

13 DO SOMETHING with one or more of your bubbles from the 12th. Write more, take it to the next small step.

14 B-day of nature writer **HAL BORLAND**, who said, "You can't be suspicious of a tree, accuse a bird or squirrel of subversion, or challenge the ideology of a violet." Take a walk and feel the purity of nature wash away the complications of being human. Write about nature's simplicity. Or play with the malleable mind and for instance, suspect a tree of following you. Write a poem about it or visually journal a stalking tree.

15 B-day of **L. FRANK BAUM** who said, "Whenever I feel blue, I start breathing again." Write about the color blue or create a picture that is made of only different shades of blue. Breathe.

16 L. Frank Baum also said, "PAY NO ATTENTION TO THAT MAN BEHIND THE CURTAIN." If there were a man behind the curtains in your world, what would he be controlling? Who is the you that you present to the world, and who is the you that you feel most comfortable being? Are they the same? If there were something else you wanted to have the man behind the curtain control, what would it be? Write, create, follow a yellow brick road (red bricks also accepted).

17 B-day of singer-songwriter, **ENYA**, who said, "I do a so-called trip into myself: I sit down at the piano and the melody might start to evolve from my playing or then I might start to sing it." What would a trip inside yourself look like? Get quiet and in a meditative mind, imagine walking into the garden of your creativity. Allow it to design itself to please you. Take at least 5 minute to fully sense all that is your garden. Then begin writing: "In the garden of my creativity . . ."

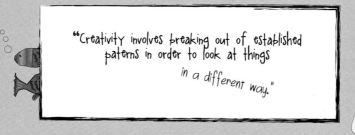

18 B-day of **TINA FEY**, who in *BossyPants* writes, "Do your thing, and don't care if they like it," and "You have to try your hardest to be at the top of your game and improve every joke you can until the last possible second, and then you have to let it go." Don't care what others think, and at some point let go–this is your formula for relaxing in the creative process today. Where can you apply this in your life? Journal about it.

19 B-day of Edward de Bono, who said,

> "Creativity involves breaking out of established paterns in order to look at things *in a different way.*"

Choose a different perspective (like the point of view of a kid, a detective, a crook, a nun, a barfly, a pirate, a street person, a librarian), and write about one or more of these topics: waking up in the morning, dancing, shopping, or your current obsession.

20 B-day of poet **W. H. AUDEN,** who wrote, "In times of joy, all of us wished we possessed a tail we could wag." Write about what your tail would look like if you had one, and make a list of all the things for which you would wag it. Or write a recent tale of joy.

21 We're not done with W.H. Auden. He also said, "All we are not stares back at what we are." Write or make art about **WHAT STARES AT YOU**.

22 B-day of painter **MARY CASSATT**. One of her most recognized paintings is *The Child's Bath*. Write or make art about taking a bath as a child or as an adult. Or take a bath and daydream about your next creative step. Add candles, music, and a beverage for a feeling of being taken care of by your creative spirit.

Cloud Architecture

23 FREE-ASSOCIATE using the word **"MAY."**

24 B-day of author **JANET WHITEHEAD**, who said, "Question anything that has you thinking you are anything less than awesome." Draw a circle. Inside of it place everything and everyone that makes you feel awesome; on the outside place things you don't need. You will notice that just the process creates an important feeling.

25 B-day of **RALPH WALDO EMERSON**, who said, "Live in the sunshine, swim the sea, drink the wild air." Continue this list with your own additions that ring with the poetry of deep living. Party with friends, laugh with the dog, dance on the table-stuff like that. Consider illustrating your list.

26 B-day of musician and writer, **SHANNON BATES**, who said, "I just remembered something I never knew." You'd be surprised what kind of poetry or ideas can emerge by making a list of things you just remembered that you never knew. Try it: Suspend logic and criticism. Possible list title: Things I Forgot But Now I Remember.

27 Make a list of what **YOUR HEART** has been through in your life and then visually depict it on a map or a timeline. Make sure you celebrate the highs as well as the heartbreaks. Consider writing little scenic marker haikus about what you learned or felt each time.

28 Find something in your house and think about it differently. **SUSPEND LOGIC** and write about what else your blender might be. Open a recipe book and let a few

words or actions inspire poetry. What funny thing would your closet say to you if it could speak? What compliment would your fridge give you?

29 B-day of **G. K. CHESTERTON** who said, "There are no rules of architecture for a castle in the clouds." But what if there were? Write a tongue-in-cheek or poignant list of rules for cloud castles, sand castles, or mirages. Photograph a series of clouds. Make a collage. Cloud up your mirror with your breath. Look at them from both sides now.

30 G. K. Chesterton also said, "If you **LOOK AT A THING** 999 times, you are perfectly safe; if you look at it for the 1000th time, you are in danger of seeing it for the first time." Imagine seeing the reflection of yourself in a restaurant mirror. Reflect on that person in writing, before you realize it's yourself. Reflect on it as if you are seeing yourself for the first time.

31 Alan Alda said, "You have to **LEAVE THE CITY OF YOUR COMFORT AND GO INTO THE WILDERNESS** of your intuition. You can't get there by bus, only by hard work and risk and by not quite knowing what you're doing, but what you'll discover will be wonderful. What you'll discover will be yourself." What have you put off because you think you need to know more before you begin? Start it and trust that the discoveries will be more vast if you rely on your intuition and not on someone else's instructions.

THEY'RE ONLY
CRAYONS. YOU DIDN'T
FEAR THEM IN
KINDERGARTEN, WHY
FEAR THEM NOW?
~HUGH MACLEOD

1 On June 1, 1824 Eugene Delacroix wrote in his journal, **LOVER OF THE MUSES**, "You who vow to their cult your purest blood, ask these learned divinities to give you back that lively eye sparkling with youth, that lightness of an untroubled mind."

If you asked your muses to give you some of your childlikeness back, which kid-like trait would you hope they'd give you and what would you do with it? Imagination, invincibility, being uninhibited?

2 B-day of writer **BARBARA PYM**, who wrote in *Excellent Women*, "My thoughts went round and round and it occurred to me that if I ever wrote a novel it would be of the 'stream of consciousness' type and deal with an hour in the life of a woman at the sink."

Begin a stream of consciousness piece about standing at the sink. Use detail about what you are thinking alternating with what you are specifically doing in the sink. Standing in front of an open fridge would work. Sink or refrigerator art is also positive.

3 B-day of poet **ALLEN GINSBERG**, who wrote, "Concentrate on what you want to say to yourself and your friends. Follow your inner moonlight; don't hide the madness. You say what you want to say when you don't care who's listening."

Discuss a response to this quote, in prose or poetry, with yourself. Make a map of your inner moonlight. Depict "madness" with doodles.

4 Write some **HAIKU.**
Open a dictionary or your window for subjects.

Sometimes I wonder
Where my Haiku would go if
it wasn't planned.

It's almost summer
Spring's just asking one more thing,
Open the window.

5 B-day of **JEAN COCTEAU**, who said, "The greatest masterpiece in literature is only a dictionary out of order."

Take a dictionary and choose a bunch of words and order them into a poem, prose, or visual collage.

6 B-day of poet **MAXINE KUMIN**.
One of her books of poetry is titled, *Where I Live*. Make this the title of a poem, a prose piece, a collage or other visual art piece that you create. Make a map of your living space with captions for various areas.

7 AND 8 IDEAS FOR DOODLING

Loosen up and doodle your favorite selection from the list below or your imagaination; consider rendering several versions of the same thing. Doodle abstract concepts–suspend logic and explore their visual essence.

DOODLE:

Free-floating freckles
A parade float
A belly button
A belly button with an attitude
A yo-yo
A yo-yo that's out of control
A Halloween ornament
A jack-o'-lantern for Valentine's Day
A cloud with sneakers
A cloud raining hugs and kisses: xoxox
A doorbell
Angst with a hat
Hesitation
Celebration
Claustrophobia
Spontaneity
A nightmare riding a bike
Calm
An award for whatever
Daisies with attitudes

A wagging tail
Confidence
Lost
Found
Your brain on creativity
Egg yolks in captivity
A bunny directing traffic

A doodle dreaming a doodle
Your creative block
Your creative block breaking up
What's on the other side of your creative block
A bunch of butterflies
A map of your inner universe
Cupcakes with weather vanes
A map of your closet
A duck with a hat
A giraffe grazing on stars
Stars in a bucket ·
A parade of suns
A doodle with a punk hairdo
A banana with sunglasses
A disassembled clock
A TV broadcasting tulips

Drawing is putting a line round an idea. ~henri Matisse

162

JUNE

9 B-day of novelist **CHARLES WEB**. He wrote *The Graduate* in the poolside bar of the Pasadena Huntington Hotel. He based it loosely on his own experience being attracted to the wife of a friend of his parents. He decided "it might be better to write about it than to do it." Write about something that is better to write about than do. Live out a fantasy in poem or prose even if it's just a short piece. (Optional: Write it poolside.)

11 B-day of actor and musician **HUGH LAURIE**, who wrote, "Now, my mom always said two wrongs don't make a right. But she never said anything about four wrongs, and that always left me confused." Write about four wrongs you feel you've done in your life and with a creative perspective, find one "right" about each of them.

12 B-day of musician **CHICK COREA**, who said, "It's very difficult for me to dislike an artist. No matter what he's creating, the fact that he's experiencing the joy of creation makes me feel like we're in a brotherhood of some kind . . . we're in it together." Decide to experience the joy of creation not only as a connection to other artists and writers, but as a connection to all that's good inside of you. Write about that connection.

13 B-day of poet **WILLIAM BUTLER YEATS**, who said, "The world is full of magic things, patiently waiting for our senses to grow sharper." Sharpen your senses and write a list of magic things in the vicinity of your existence. Write about them from the point of view of all the senses: sight, touch, taste, smell, humor.

14 B-day of **RAINER MARIA RILKE** who said, "I want to be with those who know secret things or else alone." Explore this quote in art or writing.
Answer this question using different Thinking Caps: What secret things do you know?
Thinking Caps: Fiction, science fiction, silliness, poetry, philosophical, nonsense, mysterious, annoyed, talkative, minimalistic.

15 Write a letter from your **MUSE** to yourself. Use your nondominant hand. Suggestions on how to start:

~Dear [YOUR NAME HERE], I have a little idea for you . . .

~Psst, come a little closer. There's something you should consider.

~ Hi, I'm your Muse. Here's a list of what you get to do today.

go for interesting not perfect

16 Use the Thinking Tool of **REPETITION** in prose, poetry, or visual journaling. Come up with a phrase, word, or image that you return to over and over in order to emphasize its importance or simply to create an interesting effect.

JUNE

17 SCAVENGER HUNT:
1. Open a novel (or any book if you're without novel) and grab a few phrases.
2. Open a dictionary or magazine and grab three words (or word pairs).
3. Get four verbs from a cookbook and one adjective that describes something inside your refrigerator.
4. Retrieve five random nouns from your childhood.
5. Add black.
Combine words, add more as necessary, and make poetry, prose, a litany, nonsense, a super-short story, a news report, or a secret.

18 ASK A QUESTION, write it down. Open books randomly and jot down 10 phrases or images that could be interpreted as answers. Write about it.

19 Quickly **FREE-ASSOCIATE** a mind map or list of visions, any visions–you decide. Be prolific. Make a long list, beyond your usual stopping place. Forge into new lands of visions.

20 GO BACK TO YESTERDAY and pick some of your visions. Let them be triggers for poetry, prose, art, or simple contemplation.

21 Use the same prompt Oriah Mountain Dreamer used to write **THE INVITATION**. (Google for reference.)
It's a two part fill-in-the-blank:
"It doesn't interest me . . . I want to know . . . "
It doesn't interest me how old you are. I want to know if you will risk looking like a fool for love, for your dream, for the adventure of being alive.
~Oriah Mountain Dreamer

22 B-day of author **BETHANY CRANDELL**, who said, "Some days the dog licking the dinner plates is the only help you're going to get. Just pat his head and say thanks." Write a thank you note to the dog, the cat, a friend that's helped you recently, or an imaginary friend.

23 B-day of author **ROB BRESZNY,** who wrote, "All of us need to be in touch with a mysterious, tantalizing source of inspiration that teases our sense of wonder and goads us on to life's next adventure." And "Glide through life as if all of creation is yearning to honor and entertain you."

Close your eyes, silence your mind, and get in touch with the invitation to your next Adventure, even if it's to have 5% more rowdy bliss in your next small step. Scrawl ideas on a cocktail napkin, your arm, or in your companion journal.

A photo essay on the Hanging Laundry in Italy, (tweaked slightly in Photoshop.)

24 Do a **PHOTOGRAPHIC ESSAY** even if you're not a photographer. Use the Thinking Caps on page 80. Choose one or more Thinking Caps from which to see a new perspective for your essay. Or if you don't have the equipment, write what you would do if you were making a photographic essay. What would your photos look like if you approached them absentminded, angry, sideways, in love, in a hurry? What if you focused on certain colors, textures, subjects according to one word in the alphabet?

25 Write a four-line **SHORT POEM OR HAIKU** about the moon, hanging laundry, or where you would be like to be located if you were a statue.

END OF JUNE

26 B-day of singer-songwriter **CHRIS ISAAK**. Make prose, poetry, or visual art by assembling together different words from some of his song titles: "I'm Not Waiting," "Don't Make Me Dream About You," "Shadows in a Mirror," "The End of Everything."
Add more words as needed or use them intact as titles for your own original writing or art:
Use "I'm not waiting . . ." as a repeat completion. Examples: I'm not waiting for the sky to fall or for that guy to call.

27 B-day of **HELEN KELLER**, who said many inspiring things and this lesser-known quote: "College isn't the place to go for ideas." Write a list of all the places you go for ideas and then get rambunctious and list at least 10 more places, inviting the absurd, unreal, or silly. Make an illustrated map of those places. Doodle for 7 minutes straight and then write about any ideas that come from that doodling.

28 B-day of surrealistic novelist **AIMEE BENDER**, who wrote a book called *The Particular Sadness of Lemon Cake* in which the main character can taste feelings baked into cakes and breads, feelings the people around her have but are not often aware of. Ponder in writing or thought feelings you have that might be buried. Into what foods would you bake them? Or brainstorm feelings in general and then determine to what foods you might assign them. Or be particularly happy about a cupcake.

29 B-day of **ANTOINE DE SAINT-EXUPERY**, who in *The Little Prince* wrote, "It is such a mysterious place, the land of tears."
Close your eyes and check for tears that would like to be liberated. Keep going with one of the following starters: "I have tears. . .", "Her tears . . ." or "Tears . . ."

Beauty of whatever kind, in its supreme development, invariably excites the sensitive soul to tears. —Edgar Allan Poe

When a stargirl cries, she sheds not tears but light. —Jerry Spinelli

30 WORD POOL: Combine the following words and phrases, adding more as needed to make poetry, prose, a tale about summer magic:
spells, formula, west wind, move, song, jealous sky, walked, gaze awhile, fields, fell, golden, last, trumpets, promise, softly, broken.

CREATIVE POWER IS MIGHTIER THAN ITS POSSESSOR. ~C.G. JUNG

JULY

1 Write a list of **SUMMER SENSATIONS AND FEEELINGS**: smells, tastes, sounds, textures, sights. Now go back and add more detail. Be an observer and notice what feelings emerge and capture those as well. Scan the list you've made and see what gives you the most creative juju, what wants to be a haiku, a poem, a journey into prose. Comply.

2 Take the first line of one of your **FAVORITE SONGS** and use it in a story, short prose piece, a poem, or as inspiration for visual art or photography.

3 B-day of humorist **DAVE BARRY**, who said, "The word aerobics comes from two Greek words: *aero*, meaning 'ability to,' and *bics*, meaning 'withstand tremendous boredom.'" Take some words you have feelings about, positive or negative, break them into syllables, and make up definitions for those syllables. Or do some non-boring cardio activity.

JULY 4 WILLIAM FAULKNER said, "We must be free not because we claim freedom, but because we practice it." Where do you feel the most freedom in your life? Where can you create more? What if you felt complete freedom as you created? Experience the freedom possible in a simple breath . . . it's there.

5 WORD POOL: Use some or all of the following words; add more and flow into a word journey: emerge, edgy, elongate, ethereal, underneath, land, portray, leaf, lightly, luxuriate, leap, landing, juniper, cheer, chair, lock, woman, peek, sideways, looking good, black.

6 Copy this **ERNEST HEMINGWAY** sentence and keep going with it: "My aim is to put down on paper what I see and what I feel in the best and simplest way."

7 Write a **SHORT PARAGRAPH** about something you did this week. Then write another paragraph about the same thing but this time exaggerate, consider adding fantasy, and possibly a dog.

Look with all your eyes, look.
Jules Verne

8   Novelist **AIMEE BENDER** wrote in *The Particular Sadness of Lemon Cake,* "I was with them for all of it, but more like an echo than a participant." Where have you been more like an echo than a participant? Where have you been a loud trumpet? How about song, a messenger, a burp, an alarm, a whisper? Write about or depict it.

9   B-day of noveist, **DEAN KOONTZ**, who wrote, "Every life is complicated, every mind a kingdom of unmapped mysteries."
Explore the map of your mysteries by completing one or more of these phrases quickly at least 10 times:
● I wonder why I . . .
● My mind is . . .
● The map of my life leads . . .
If one of the completions calls to you for more investigation, image depiction, or decision making, ignore resistance and follow through.
 If you have an epiphany, e-mail me and tell me about it.

10   B-day of **MARCEL PROUST**, who wrote, "His nature was really like a sheet of paper that has been folded so often in every direction that it is impossible to straighten it out."
Make a list of some of the ways you see yourself, (both positive and negative), then come up with items that may be compared to your nature. Use household objects, office supplies, kitchen utensils, nature, a doodle, and write about it. Don't worry about making complete sense, just pick items that seem to intuitively have a story about some of who you are.
This is a maintenance tool for using the über creative practice of making associations as well as discovering a unique definition of yourself.

11 Our **HAIR** is filled with stories (and mine also has several goop products in it). There are classic bad-hair days, how we feel about our hair, transitions it's made. Write a quick story, poem, or hair-ku. (I caught mine on fire at a candlelight church service once.) Have your hair write to you or about you. Write a news story or a how-to about your hair. Write a short history of your hair.

12 B-day of **BUCKMINSTER FULLER**, who said, "Dare to be naïve."
Naïveté is a characteristic of creative people. Suspending influence from past experiences, staying open to possibilities without cynicism, letting go of the ego's need to know everything. Take a moment and see if you can recapture simplicity. Write with wonder about the weather today.

13 Write four haikus with these subjects: cats, dogs, birds, and fish. Or you come up with four of your own subjects.

14 B-day of **WOODY GUTHRIE**, who said, "Any fool can make something complicated. It takes a genius to make it simple." Take one of your Creative Adventures and ask, How can I make this simpler? Fill in this repeat-completion at least five times: "It would be simpler to . . ."

15 Write just the **FIRST LINE** of a novel, a memoir, or a poem.

16 B-day of playwright, **TONY KUSHNER**, who wrote in *Angels in America*, "Don't be afraid; people are so afraid; don't be afraid to live in the raw wind, naked, alone . . . . Learn at least this: What you are capable of. Let nothing stand in your way." I have nothing to add, 'cept: "Yeah, find your definition of the raw wind and get naked." Imagine it now. Oh, and if you want to write or draw something, doing that would show fear a thing or two, wouldn't it?

17 B-day of comedienne, **PHYLLIS DILLER**, according to the *Writer's Almanac*, "She didn't start her career in stand-up comedy until she was middle-aged. But she had spent much of her life as a housewife, telling jokes and doing impersonations and making groups of people laugh. At the laundromat, she would tell other housewives things like, 'I bury a lot of my ironing in the backyard' and 'Housework can't kill you, but why take a chance?'" Write a fictional (or non-fictional) account of what you would bury or what is buried in your backyard.

18 B-day of **HUNTER S. THOMPSON** who said, "Buy the ticket, take the ride." What ride? Mind-map metaphorical "rides" you'd like to take. Write a haiku or poem about the ticket. Use mixed media to make a ticket for a journey of some sort.

19 Take **5 MINUTES** today, set a timer, and make progress on something that you need to do to free up more creative energy. Pay a bill, clean the cat box, make that call. Make it a game. Pretend like this is a special mission and completing it not only will feel good, but will result in a special award. Looming chores steal creative juju. I'm holding the space for you to do this . . . and I'm going to do it, too.

20 Word Trigger: **RECLINE**. Interpret intuitively… write or otherwise create anything the word "recline" triggers. Free-associate. Daydream. Or word pool. Use these words, add more as needed: bend, believe, burden, bewilder, beneath, bellow, bougainvillea, birdbath, and bring.

21 B-day of **ERNEST HEMINGWAY**, who said, "The first draft of anything is shit." Write a first draft of anything: A poem, a page in a memoir, an essay, an outline for a work of brilliance. Add fun.

22 B-day of **TOM ROBBINS**, who said, "Curiosity, especially intellectual inquisitiveness, is what separates the truly alive from those who are merely going through the motions." Write a poem or create art around what you are curious about. Repeatedly fill in this sentence and see where it goes: "Well, I am curious about . . ."

23 WORD POOL: Play with these words and phrases: Come with me, separate universe, wild, flame, stumbling, fragments, hummingbird, dark song, fluttering, touch, something real.

24 B-day of **JOHN D. MACDONALD**, who said, "My purpose is to entertain myself first and other people secondly." Ponder how this quote might inspire the next step of your Creative Adventure. What if your next step was all about just entertaining yourself?

25 B-day of novelist and playwright **ELIAS CANETTI**. In *The Human Province* (1978), he wrote: "His head is made of stars, but not yet arranged into constellations." If your head were arranged into a constellation, what figure would it be? If you want, make a list of all of the possibilities and then choose one to write about.

26 MY BIRTHDAY. "Am I supposed to say something here? It's my birthday, may I have the day off?" Take the day off. Buy a new outfit. I do every year on this day, so you have permission to do so too. C. G. Jung was also born today.

27 Take a moment and write a reminder about **SOMETHING THAT'S WORKING**, or something important you've learned in this book. Post it on your fridge, memorize it, or say out it loud in an Irish accent (deep Southern would work too).

28 I can't expect that you've been doing these prompts every day. That's unrealistic. **GO BACK** and pick one you haven't done, or do the next step of something you've started. Or edit, modify, or personify something.

29 B-day of **STANLEY KUNITZ,** who became the poet laureate when he was ninety-five. About poetry he wrote, "You must be careful not to deprive the poem of its wild origin." He also wrote, "End with an image and don't explain." Write a poem with a wild origin, (something written in haste, something from unanalyzed passion) and end with some image you don't explain. Make a collage that defies explanation.

30 B-day of *Wuthering Heights* author **EMILY BRONTE**, who wrote "I have dreamed in my life, dreams that have stayed with me ever after, and changed my ideas; they have gone through and through me, like wine through water, and altered the color of my mind." Close your eyes and allow a creative essence of life, like wonder or imagination, to go through you. Imagine and feel it change the color of your mind. Render it in art and poetry; give it a title.

31 B-day of Harry Potter author, **J. K. ROWLING** who wrote, "I solemnly swear that I am up to no good." Write your own Doctrine of Mischievousness. J. K. also wrote:

"Don't put your wand in your back pocket! Better wizards than you have lost buttocks from it."

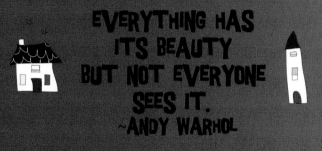

EVERYTHING HAS
ITS BEAUTY
BUT NOT EVERYONE
SEES IT.
~ANDY WARHOL

AUGUST MAINTENANCE

AUGUST

1 B-day of **HERMAN MELVILLE**, who wrote in *Moby Dick*, "It is not down on any map; true places never are." Free-associate a list or a mind-map of true places, however you interpret that term. Write about one as if you were a travel writer noting scenery, hot spots, main attractions, and accommodations. Or write three haiku about true places. Or just BE a true place.

2 B-day of **ISABELLE ALLENDE**, who wrote, "And I am not one of those women who trips twice over the same stone." Journey into your past and write or visually depict in doodles, collage, or painting the stones you've tripped over once, twice, or even more, and then depict and title the ones you are stepping on, to advance forward into joy and laughter.

3 B-day of author **ALEX BOSWORTH**, who describes his process: "For thirty-five years, my method has rarely varied. I grab an absurd concept like a loose football and charge forward, gaining as much creative yardage as I can. From unique theories arrived at by my niece about how nature operates, to a simple misinterpretation of a newspaper headline, each peculiar notion provides me with a premise for an equally bizarre plot. The characters, on the other hand, are all stolen from Dickens."
Steal a character from a classic story and write about sharing a burger with him or her, get their opinion about a decision you need to make, or create a scene or dialogue between a group of characters from different stories.

4 Photographer **DIANE ARBUS** wrote: "I work from awkwardness. By that I mean I don't like to arrange things. If I stand in front of something, instead of arranging it, I arrange myself." Try it. Stand in front of a lamp, a garden, your kitchen sink, your sweetheart, a difficult person, and arrange yourself. Write or create art as a response. Or cut out a bunch of images and rearrange them at least three different ways, writing a short description about each one.

5 B-day of writer **GUY DE MAUPASSANT**, who said, "Our memory is a more perfect world than the universe: it gives back life to those who no longer exist." Write a list of favorite memories, if only for the reason of reliving the joy they gave you. If you don't want to go back, write a few projected memories you would LIKE to have for events that haven't happened yet. Illustrate in a collage.

6 B-day of **ALFRED, LORD TENNYSON**, who wrote, "The words 'far, far away' had always a strange charm." Write, create art, or photograph a piece that depicts far, far away. Or quickly repeat, "Far, far away . . ." filling it in differently each time until you hit on a completion that you want to continue with.

7 B-day of essayist and book lover **ANNE FADIMAN**, who said, "In my view, nineteen pounds of old books are at least nineteen times as delicious as one pound of fresh caviar." And "If you truly love a book, you should sleep with it, write in it, read aloud from it, and fill its pages with muffin crumbs."
Do you have a beloved book? Show it a little love by writing a poem about it, carrying it around a bit, and reading it while eating a banana chocolate-chip muffin (or one of YOUR favorites). Or put crumbs in a book and with the words that the crumbs choose, write a poem.

8 B-day of writer **MARJORIE KINNAN RAWLINGS,** who wrote "I do not understand how anyone can live without some small place of enchantment to turn to." Write or create art about small places of enchantment. In addition to describing one you have, or ones you've had, invent one. Describe it in full detail. Invent what's not there and embellish it with your imagination.

AUGUST

9 Mark Twain said, "When I'm playful I use the meridians of longitude and parallels of latitude for a seine, and drag the Atlantic Ocean for whales. **I SCRATCH MY HEAD** with the lightning and purr myself to sleep with the thunder." Write something using the same spirit of grandeur and fantasy, begin with, "When I'm playful . . ."

10 B-day of my mom. She used to always say to me, "**YOU'RE SILLY.**" To immortalize my momism, I made a collage coincidentally titled, "You're Silly." It was a daughter-mom thing. Feel free to do one with that title, too. Or consider what your mom used to say or still says, whether it felt good or made you wonder about her or yourself. Make collages, paintings, or poems based on that inspiration. Momisms are part of your fabric, interpret them artfully to either treasure your mom's words or heal your feelings about them.

11 Writer **EDITH WHARTON** left the planet on this day. She said, "Set wide the window. Let me drink the day." Look out any window and write about or artistically render what you see. If you write, use great detail. If you do art, try an abstract, a doodle, or using your nondominant hand. And have a sip of afternoon.

12 You have permission to **RESIGN** as General Manager of the universe today. Take the day off from trying to be in control and being a better person. Believe that you're fine the way you are. Relax. Breathe. Buy a popsicle.

13 B-day of author **MARNEY MADRIDAKIS**, who wrote in *Creating Time*, "We create time when we pause our rushing mind for a moment to connect with the intricate and fanciful work of art that we ourselves create each and every day, as we step into the full grandeur of possibility and wonder that time holds." If "possibility" were to write you a letter, what would it say?

14 B-day of humorist **RUSSELL BAKER**, who said, "Life is always walking up to us and saying, 'Come on in, the living's fine,' and what do we do? Back off and take its picture." Find a place in nature today and be a part of its life without having to do anything extra.

15 B-day of poet **MARY JO SALTER**, who in an interview said, "Every once in a while I'll realize that I really have written some version of that poem before. So I do want to try new things and new angles. I find that reading other writers who are unlike myself is one of the best ways to jumpstart." So, maybe you could try that with writing, art, or photography too. Just sayin'.

16 B-day of **CHARLES BUKOWSKI** who wrote,
> "Nothing can save
> you except writing.
> It keeps the walls from failing."

Expose yourself to Bukowski today, save yourself—wax poetically. Feed your writing passion by liberating some soul-driven words. Or write about the walls.

17 B-day of poet **TED HUGHES**, who said, "You are who you choose to be." Make a list of who you've chosen to be. Suggested categories: roles, beliefs, strengths, shadows. Or write three short haikus instead. Or perhaps a memoir beginning with the first line. "I have chosen to be . . ."

18 **PAUL RUDNICK** said, "Writing is 90 percent procrastination: reading magazines, eating cereal out of the box, watching infomercials."
Sometimes when you think you are procrastinating, there's a chance you are actually incubating. When you relax and believe that allowing some diversion is okay, the juices may flow more easily once you are ready to begin than if you are constantly berating yourself about not getting to the work. How can you relax and trust the process today? What cereal would you eat out of the box? What would you write on the back of a cereal box?
What percolator question can you ask about your next creative step?

AUGUST

19 B-day of poet **OGDEN NASH,** who said, "If called by a panther, don't anther." Today play with finishing this sentence in several different ways:
"If called . . . " If you find one response you really like, illustrate it or write more from it. Or make a list of things, ideas or people who if they called, you would answer.

20 WORD POOL: Write a dog-days poem or prose piece using these words and phrases, adding more as you need them: reason, circle, give a little, forget, chair, any, poplar, meander, born, lying, avenue, quiz, write, track, design, place ladder, troubled, mistake, find, accept, branch, swing, foot, dog day.

21 DAYDREAM AND DOODLE:
Return to June 7 if you need doodling ideas.

22 B-day of writer **DOROTHY PARKER,** who got kicked out of Catholic school for describing the Immaculate Conception as "spontaneous combustion." Fantasize about getting kicked out of someplace even if it would never happen. Where would you like to be kicked out of, fictionally or in reality? Write a haiku, a poem, or an account in the local paper about getting kicked out. Kick your inner critic out.

23 MARK TWAIN said, "When I was younger I could remember anything, whether it had happened or not." Write about something that didn't happen as if you remembered it did, or illustrate his quote with visual journaling and photos of you pasted on other people's bodies. Or find a picture in a magazine or online and write about it as if it were a memory of yours.
Begin: "Oh yes, I remember . . . "

24 Take a **LINE** from a favorite novel and let it inspire art, free associating, photography, collage, music, movement. Here are some to choose from in case you don't want to get up and find a novel:

"Ships at a distance have every man's wish on board." ~Zora Neale Hurston

"I write this sitting in the kitchen sink." ~Dodie Smith

25 TITLES: Mix them together, use just one or all as catalysts for poetry, story, collage, or paintings:
Whisper to Me, From the Sky, Odd Soul, Tell Your Heart Heads Up, Words Meet Heart Beats, Mediocre Bad Guys, Rusty Halo, Wrong End of the Rainbow.

26 Take one of the following **SONG** titles and use it for a title for poetry, prose, a visual journal page, or painting:
"The One That Got Away" by Tom Waits
"The Horizon Has Been Defeated" by Jack Johnson
"The Man Who Can't Be Moved" by The Script

27 Use these titles of paintings and songs as **RAW MATERIALS** for free-associating, combining, or as titles for your own writing or art:
From Nancy Farmer: *Medusa and the Hairdryer, A Rude Intrusion*
From Sandra Gotautaite: *Before Falling Asleep*
From Tom Rush: "Trolling for Owls"

28 Take this Greg Kuzma quote, "Hold the **MAP** close to your face. Breathe into it and hear a river start" and keep going with it in writing. What happens next? Let it inspire art. Or hold a map close to your face and see what ideas run free.

29 Time for some **SUMMER-TIME PLAY**. Complete this unfinished sentence once or more: "Right here in front of me . . ." Keep going with the completion that has the most juice.

30 WEAR A COSTUME, SPECIAL HAT, OR ACCESSORY as you paint, write, daydream, or otherwise create and act as if it is endowed with special powers to help you create easier or break through resistance. Believe in the creative potential of acting "as if . . ." and pretending.

31 Write a **POETRY OR PROSE** piece that uses a lot of words that begin with the letter

romance ring retro

EVERY ARTIST HAS THOU-
SANDS OF BAD
DRAWINGS IN THEM AND
THE ONLY WAY TO GET RID
OF THEM IS TO DRAW
THEM OUT.
~CHUCK JONES

SEPTEMBER MAINTENANCE

SEPTEMBER

1 W.H. AUDEN wrote a poem that became famous called *September First*. Keep going with his first line but take it in your own direction:
"I sit in one of the dives on Fifty-second Street . . ."

2 PERCOLATOR QUESTIONS:
If you're the arrow what is the target?
What are you glad you did yesterday?
What you going to be glad you did at this time next week?
What's the title of your cookbook?
If you were a poem, what would be the first line?
If you were a figure in a landscape what would that landscape be?
If there was a note with 4 words on it stuck to your forehead, what would it say?

3 Continue the prompt from yesterday. Develop some of the ideas, thoughts, or images you received from **DOING THE CREATIVITY WALK.** Or try another walk. Or go back to any prompt that needs more work or a fresh perspective and work on it some more.

4 B-day of writer **RICHARD WRIGHT**, who said, "The artist must bow to the monster of his own imagination." Depict the monster of your imagination in a doodle, a collage, a poem, or a How-to Bow to the Monster of Your Imagination article. Free-associate: Imagination-Monsters.
Also bow to the chameleon, the guppie, the angel, and the busboy of your imagination.

5 B-day of composer, philosopher, poet, artist **JOHN CAGE**. To compose a piece of music, Cage would come up with questions to ask the *I Ching,* (an ancient Chinese classic text on changing events). What book or resource meant for one thing can be a source of inspiration for another things? Ask a question and find an answer in a gardening guide, cook-book, songbook, a book of poems or quotes. Walk through a bookstore and open several books and compile answers in a poem or clever report.

6 PONDER: What prompt have you really enjoyed so far? Do it again a little differently. What's been working for you in general? Perhaps you might consider continuing to do it.

7 B-day of author **JENNIFER EGAN**, who wrote in her book, *A Visit from the Goon Squad*, "It's turning out to be a bad day, a day when the sun feels like teeth." Good art and writing work off of metaphors. Practice: Make a list of subjects like sun, love, a visit home, work, doubt, a relationship, and then brainstorm what those things are like. Don't worry about getting it exactly right; invite the absurd, and be more concerned with quantity than quality.

8 B-day of singer-songwriter **AIMEE MANN**, who wrote a song called, "I Can't Help You Anymore." Use this as a title of a poem, story, or journal entry. Consider doing it more than once, talking to more than one person.

9 B-day of **LEO TOLSTOY**, who wrote in *Anna Karenina*, "Rummaging in our souls, we often dig up something that ought to have lain there unnoticed." The quote is great inspiration for a mixed-media piece, a poem, a journal entry, or a ritual for discovering something unsavory and rising above it. Rummage through your soul and find three things you really like. Portray in poetry or art.

10 B-day of writer **MARY OLIVER**. Take this sentence of hers and keep going with it in your own direction: "I don't want to end up simply having visited this world."

11 Complete this phrase very quickly several times: "**DID I EVER TELL YOU ABOUT THE TIME** …" Then pick one of the completions and keep writing about it, but experiment with one or more of the following: Write about yourself in second or third person, use a long run-on sentence, use short little poetic sentences, use lots of details, get dark, be upbeat, write a really bad version, exaggerate, write about it as if you are going to do it tomorrow, find a moral to the story, write as if it were a screenplay with stage directions, and/or start at the end of the story.

Note to self Stare at a cloud until Your mind is clear.

September

12 To create an experience of **APPRECIATION** through creativity's back-door, make a list of 12 things you want (but make them things you already have).

13 B-day of **ROALD DAHL** who said, "Do you know what breakfast cereal is made of? It's made of all those little curly wooden shavings you find in pencil sharpeners!" Dahl suspended logic to liberate imagination. Make a list of imaginative ingredients for real things like pillows, cameras, angst, eagerness, paranoia, altruism. See if your exploration leads to ideas for writing or art, or just let it strengthen your imagination muscles.

14 **SNOOP AROUND** and check out your creative projects as if you were a snooping housesitter. Notice if seeing it from this point of view helps you appreciate your work differently. Write about the experience as the housesitter or as you. Consider starting with: "Interesting! I was snooping and came across . . . "

15 SCAVENGER HUNT:

Open a favorite novel (or any bookl), and grab a few phrases.
Open a dictionary or magazine and grab three words (or word pairs).
Extract four verbs from a cookbook and one adjective describing something in your refrigerator. Retrieve five random nouns from your childhood.
Add black. Use all in a piece of writing or art.

16 SCAVENGER HUNT TOO:

Find two images.
Look in a junk drawer for two objects.
Turn on the TV or radio and capture a line or two of dialog or reporting.
Make a cup of tea (for drinking), but if there's a word or phrase on the box of tea, grab that too).
Use all to inspire a piece of writing, direction for a work of art, or just enjoy as a novel activity.

17 SCAVENGER HUNT THREE

Grab two to four objects and let them inspire a short little story, poetry, a still life photograph, or laughter. Or just launch into some writing or art if one of them lends a charge of inspiration.
Or use one of these examples:
• a lemon, a tissue, an origami box, and a map
• a key, a newspaper, a cupcake, and a light bulb
• a wadded up piece of paper, a flashlight, a kaleidoscope, a color swatch
• a watch, a wine glass, a branch, a piece of paper with a phone number on it

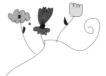

18, 19, 20 For the next three days, **FIND FAVORITE QUOTES** and personalize them:

Examples:

"There is only one of you in all time, this expression is unique. And if you block it, it will never exist through any other medium and it will be lost." ~Martha Graham

"There is only one of me in all time, my expression is unique. And if I block it, it will never exist through any other medium and it will be lost. The hell if I'm going to let that happen! " ~Jill Badonsky, as inspired by Martha Graham
****
"When the world wearies and society ceases to satisfy, there is always the garden." ~Minnie Aumonier

'When I am weary and worried, cranky, fraught with mood swings, chocolate cravings, hormonal rage, and the world is getting on my nerves, there is always my dancing imagination. There is also great literature, great beauty, great friends and of course, chocolate. Gardens are nice, too. ~Jill, as inspired by Minnie Aumonier
 ****

21 B-day of **LEONARD COHEN**, who wrote, "I cannot understand why my arm is not a lilac tree." Practice writing by repeat completing this sentence, suspending logic, inviting the absurd, being a kid, adding a slant, and believing in your cleverness: "I cannot understand . . ."
See if one of those completions begs for more writing or art.
I cannot understand why more people don't cease the merry moment and create up a storm.

22 B-day of humorist, **FRANK SULLIVAN**.
Two of his book titles are, *A Pearl in Every Oyster* and *A Rock in Every Snowball*. Keep going with associated modifications using his titles as examples, such as: *A Purr in Every Cat*, *A Prize in Every Box*, *A Poem in Every Angst*, etc. and see if you come up with titles to poems, paintings, or visual journal pages. Or just make the list itself a work of art.

SEPTEMBER

23 B-day of poet **CHRIS VANNOY**, who said about his creative process, "There is no process. It is complete chaos. Some sound (sight) catches my mind and leads me on a journey of discovery of word crafting and roller coaster ride never knowing just what is around the next bend of words and spell checking is after the fact." Chris co-wrote a book of poems called *Twenty Poems Against Love and A Song For The Air*. Write a song, a haiku, poem, or story against love or one for the air. Write it with complete chaos.

24 When writer and, filmmaker **MIRANDA JULY** procrastinated while trying to write a movie, she read the classifieds pamphlet, *The Penny Saver*, cover to cover. She ended up writing a book called, *It Chooses You*, where she called and interviewed people selling their prized possessions. Make a list of all the activities you use to procrastinate. They all have potential to be used for something creative. Assign possible project ideas to them even if you don't plan on following through. The idea generation is good practice and you may stumble on something brilliant.

25 B-day of artist/author **SHEL SILVERSTEIN**, who once wrote, "I am writing these poems from inside a lion . . ." List imaginative locations where you could write. Pick one or two and imagine how acting as if you were in those locations would shift your approach to your work. Then shift your approach.

26 B-day of poet **T. S. ELIOT**, who said, "If you haven't the strength to impose your own terms upon life, then you must accept the terms it offers you." Entitle a piece of writing or art: "My Own Terms." Play with what your terms for living might be with delightfully peculiar possibilities. Then use it for the rest of your life, with occasional revisions.

27 B-day of former poet laureate **KAY RYAN**, who wrote, "Action creates/a taste/for itself." Movement begets more movement in the creative process. Pick any project and set a timer to work of it for just five minutes without a plan other than following your intuition. Pay attention to what happens.

i am writing from the inside of a vase

28 B-day of **HENRI-FREDERIC AMIEL,** who said, "The man who has no inner life is a slave to his surroundings." Look at what's surrounding you in your life. Is any part of it imprisoning you? What would you like to surround you? (Write a list). Write or depict in doodle or art, different surroundings. What do they look like? Forest, mountain, room with a view? A crowd of unconditionally loving guides? Elves? Muses? Cabana boys? Close your eyes right now and see what's waiting for you in the magnificence and refuge of your inner world. Even if it's for only 15 seconds.

29 Paulo Coelho wrote, "The **SIMPLE THINGS** are also the most extraordinary things, and only the wise can see them." Mind-map, list, or write about the simple things in your life, or pick one and honor it in art.

30 B-day of **W. S. MERWIN,** who wrote: "Your absence has gone through me like thread through a needle. Everything I do is stitched with its color." Flip it over: Write about people whose presence in your life adds to the fabric of your joy. Other things to write about: A pattern of yours that you admire. What issues are you skirting around? What or who feels unseamly in your life right now? What needs to be ripped out and replaced?

THE HIGHEST PRIZE WE
CAN RECEIVE FOR
CREATIVE WORK
IS THE JOY OF BEING
CREATIVE.
~MARIANNE WILLIAMSON

OCTOBER
MAINTENANCE

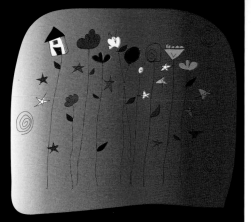

OCTOBER

1 B-day of **JULIE ANDREWS** who said, "Some people regard discipline as a chore. For me, it is a kind of order that sets me free to fly." Have you considered how discipline might be considered freedom?

When you are disciplined to show up for your Creative Adventure you free yourself from imprisoning habits and the feeling that you are doing everything but that which truly calls to you.

When disciplined, you develop the skills that result in the freedom to confidently express your ideas, take creative risks, and believe in yourself.

2 B-day of **GROUCHO MARX**, who said, "If you're not having fun, you're doing some-thing wrong." Discipline is easier when you make it fun. Make a list of intentions but make them sound fun, find 5 minutes of time to show up. Show up frequently at the same time and discipline becomes a habit.

3 B-day of **JAMES HERRIOT,** who said, "Cats are connoisseurs of comfort." Act as if, in this very moment, you, yourself, were an expert on comfort. Mind-map "comfort."

Make a list of everything that comforts you, then make it into a poem list, a collage, or a reminder. Or just make yourself comfortable, and buy some Halloween socks with cats on them.

4 B-day of **ROY BLOUNT, JR.**, who said, "If there is one thing that I pride myself on, it is this, that I have done more different things, for money, than any other humorist-novelist-journalist-dramatist-lyricist-lecturer--reviewer- performer- versifier-cruciverbalist-sportswriter-screenwriter-anthologist-columnist-philologist-biographer of sorts, that I can think of offhand." String together all of your roles to make a similar title for yourself; feel free to embellish it with some funny or absurd additions.

5 B-day of **NEIL DEGRASSE TYSON**, who said, "When I look up at the night sky, and I know that, yes we are part of this universe, we are in this universe, but perhaps more important than both of those fact is that the universe is in us." Sometimes just reading a beautiful thought is enough for a day. Close your eyes and feel all things beautiful about the universe that are inside of you.

6 B-day of novelist **CAROLINE GORDON**, who said, "A well-composed book is a magic carpet on which we are wafted to a world that we cannot enter in any other way."

Reread something that inspires you, be fully present, and see if you can waft to another world. If not, waft on your own. Make a poetic list of other ways you are wafted or transported blissfully. To exercise your creative fluency muscles, associate puns twith the word "waft," (e.g. He who wafts last . . .)

7 Keep going with this incomplete sentence: "**THE GIRL ON THE ROOF** . . . " Or write from the point of view of being on a roof and reveal where you are without saying anything about the roof.

8 B-day of writer **R. L. STINE**, who said, "Read. Read. Read. Just don't read one type of book. Read different books by various authors so that you develop different styles."

Make a list of styles and see if any excite you. Fiip through books with styles different from your own in a bookstore for the creative value of exposure. Pick three lines from page 88 in three different books and see if you can combine them and keep going with them, or choose one and keep going.

9 B-day of writer **JAMES HOWE**, who wrote in *Totally Joe*, "Life is short and there will always be dirty dishes, so let's dance."

Use the quote as inspiration for a visual journal page, or keep going with it in writing according to how it inspires you. Or don't do anything but dance.

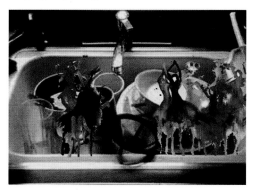

Creativity coach, Donna Mullholland's watercolor muses dance on my dirty dish photo-collage.

ALSO OCTOBER

10 Playwright, **ALAN BENNETT** said, "I often wanted to be bolder than I was, and as I've got older it's bothered me less what people think . . . I've been able to be much more outrageous, really."
Close your eyes and imagine being just 15% more outrageous. Write a list, might want to open your eyes to do this, about five ways you could be more outrageous with:
1) your Creative Adventure, 2) any relationship you have, 3) your work, 4) your looks, 5) where you live, or 6) dinner tonight.

11 B-day of **ELEANOR ROOSEVELT,** who said, "With the new day comes new strength and new thoughts." Free-associate some new thoughts, write what comes to mind, or make art that illustrates the word, "**STRONG**."

12 B-day of playwright and novelist **ALICE CHILDRESS**. Her grandmother encouraged her to write. She would sit at the window and point to people passing by and ask Alice what she thought they were thinking. Alice would make something up, and her grandmother would say,
"Now, write that down. That sounds like something we should keep." Create a benevolent grandmother in your head that says things like that to you. People-watch with a pad of paper and write down what you think people are thinking–It's great practice for strengthening creative muscles. Invite a friend, bring a picnic, and make it a grand and mirth-filled afternoon.

13 B-day of comedian **LENNY BRUCE**. Bruce developed a new form of comedy where he just stood on stage and talked about things like politics, society, religion, and race; and he free-associated on those topics to make people laugh. Free-associate on one or more of these words or phrases without worrying about being funny; go for quantity:
diaper, the produce section, neighbor's yard, under your bed, halloween costumes gone bad, halloween candy rituals, pranks, the history of stains on your clothes, embarassing moments, what the cat dragged in, arguments that ended with laughter, forts, road trips, or something unexpected that happened when company was over.

14 B-day of poet **E.E. CUMMINGS,** who wrote, "may came home with a smooth round stone as small as a world and as large as alone." Write as least three lines that rhyme within themselves. I know you can do it, just simply intuit.

15 B-day of **P.G. WODEHOUSE,** who wrote about one of his characters: "He felt like a man who, chasing rainbows, has had one of them suddenly turn and bite him in the leg." Write about having a rainbow bite you in the leg, or personify a rainbow any other way, including visually depicting a rainbow in a place doing something a rainbow wouldn't normally do.

16 What if you put your ear up against a wall and heard people talking about you? What would you hear them say? Write a scenario where this is happening. Consider writing it more than once having different people (or pets, fictional characters, relative or friends) **TALK ABOUT YOU.** Possibly even include YOU talking about you. Begin with: "When I put my ear up to the wall . . ."

17 JUST SHOW UP. A writer determined to write, sat her family down and told them, "I love you. You are important to me. But so is writing. And I can't write when you interrupt me. So it's your choice. I can either stay at home and write or rent a space and write or go to a coffee house to write. But know that I am going to do whatever is necessary to keep on writing." Imagine being that dedicated; imagine being just 5% more dedicated than you already are now. Think about what you might do with your next five minutes with that dedication.

18 CREATIVITY thrives on acting "as if" you are creative. Halloween is an "act as if" you are something or someone else kind of holiday. Celebrate the power of pretending today by pretending you are a famous creative person and writing about it. Start with, "I am . . ." And then add, "what makes me famous is the way I . . .".

OCTOBER
CONTINUES

19 When poet **SHARON OLDS,** was asked where she got the inspiration for her poems she replied, "Poems come from ordinary experiences and objects, I think. Out of memory–a dress I lent my daughter on her way back to college; a newspaper photograph of war; a breast self-exam; the tooth fairy; Calvinist parents who beat up their children; a gesture of love; seeing oneself naked over age fifty in a set of bright hotel bathroom mirrors."

Make your own list of places from which poems come for you and get specific. For instance: Poems come from wondering what that look meant, from the way my cat swats me as sport, from the quiet in the canyon below. And if one of those places invites you in, write or make art about it.

20 SELF-KINDNESS replenishes creative energy. Do something kind for yourself today. Fresh flowers, an hour of free time, allow your meditative wonder to wander. No demands.

21 B-day of musician **DIZZY GILLESPIE,** who said, "I don't care too much about music. What I like is sounds." Make a list of sounds you like, then a list of sounds you don't like. Choose one or more of your listed sounds and let it arouse poetry, prose, or stretch your imagination and define a sound in collage.

Lamppost
post
with
wings
and a
sun

22 B-day of **DORIS LESSING,** who said, "I write because I've always written, can't stop. I am a writing animal. The way a silkworm is a silk-producing animal." Give yourself the title of writer or artist and then do what people with those titles do. If you need an idea to play with, spin off of the word "spin," with free-associations and images.

23 B-day of Running with Scissors author, **AUGUSTEN BURROUGHS,** who said, "The secret to being a writer is that you have to write. It's not enough to think about writing or to study literature or plan a future life as an author. You really have to lock yourself away, alone, and get to work." Let your inspiration dash about in poetry, prose, or art using various meanings of the word "run" as a trigger. And lock yourself away alone from time to time.

24 What if the **CEILING OF YOUR LIMITATIONS** flew off?
What would you do next? What would it look like? Make art or write about it.

25 B-day of author **ANNE TYLER,** who said, "I want to live other lives. I've never quite believed that one chance is all I get. Writing is my way of making other chances. It's lucky I do it on paper. Probably I would be schizophrenic — and six times divorced—if I weren't writing."

Choose another life you would have led, and in that persona make a creative journal entry or write a poem, letting a different choice of words and moods than you would use in your current life paint the picture of this other person.

Or simply use writing as the release you need today.

26 B-day of author **BERYL MARKHAM,** who wrote in *West with the Night*: "It is amazing what a lot of insect life goes on under your nose when you have got it an inch from the earth. I suppose it goes on in any case, but if you are proceeding on your stomach, dragging your body along by your fingernails, entomology presents itself very forcibly as a thoroughly justified science."

Go find worlds that you would normally not notice–get within inches of nature. Or traverse a grocery store with hyper awareness instead of habitual half-consciousness. See the colors, the designs, labeling, or something you never bother looking at. This is an exercise in moving from the noncreative world of the automatic thinking to the myriad discoveries only possible when you are paying close attention and are awake to the moment.

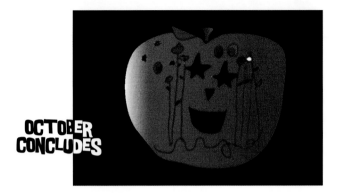

OCTOBER CONCLUDES

27 B-day of poet **DYLAN THOMAS**, who said, "When one burns one's bridges, what a very nice fire it makes." Some of the bridges you burned have turned out to be for your own good. Conjure them up and write haiku and nonjudgmental accounts of burned bridges as if they were scientific studies, or make them into little stories with unexpected morals.

28 B-day of **BILL GATES**. When he was in the eighth grade, Gates and his friend Paul Allen got completely swept up in the excitement of computer equipment that was bought for the school by the Seattle Lakeside Mothers Club from rummage sale proceeds. They rummaged through dumpsters at the nearby Computer Center Corporation to find notes written by programmers, and with that information, they wrote a 300-page manual. Dig through a dumpster or your old journals and find some parts of a poem, info that can be made into a wacky manual, new poetry, or found-objects for art. Or pretend like you did and write about it.

29 B-day of the children's poet and novelist **VALERIE WORTH**. She's most famous for her "small poems," for children about everyday objects. She said, "As a child, I was greatly attracted to 'smallness,' perhaps because throughout grade school I myself was the smallest in my class."
Write at least 4 small poems (3 to 6 lines) about everyday objects around you, such as a chair, a spoon, dust bunnies, a lamp, the welcome mat.

30 B-day of poet and critic **EZRA POUND**, who said, "The only thing one can give an artist is leisure in which to work. To give an artist leisure is actually to take part in his creation." Think about this quote in terms of how important it is for you to make time for your creative work. When you are distracted by other things, simply ask yourself, "Is this as important as my creative work?" Where can you give yourself at least 15 minutes to begin or continue a Creative Adventure? Put the book down and do it now, (then come back).

31 HALLOWEEN B-day of poet Annie Finch. An interviewer asked her how she would explain what a poem is to a 7-year-old, and she said,

> A POEM IS WORDS
> THAT FIT TOGETHER
> IN A SPECIAL WAY SO
> IT'S EASY TO
> REMEMBER
> AND IT SOUNDS LIKE
> MAGIC

Fit the following words together and add more to make something that sounds like the first draft of magic: sinister, blustery, snickers, music, shift, alarm, fine, wander, thump, drain, pop, where, wolf, there, boo.

Write a Halloween poem, but then challenge yourself to get creative, and use these Halloween-oriented words to write a poem completely unrelated to Halloween.

Permission to write **PURPOSELY BAD POETRY**.
Poem by writer and producer Steve Fix, a self-professed non-poet:
"On a moonlit night, my thoughts. Were disjointed at best. Wish I never licked that damn toad. Now I must–no matter what. Find a 7-11. I need a burrito."
(Bad poetry can actually turn out to be quite entertaining.)

Write an acronym or acrostic for **SCREAM**. Here's Vergil Den's acrostic:

Start writing
Cross the whole thing out
Restart,
Erase again what was just written
Another freakin' distraction keeps me from concentrating
My goodness where has the day gone.

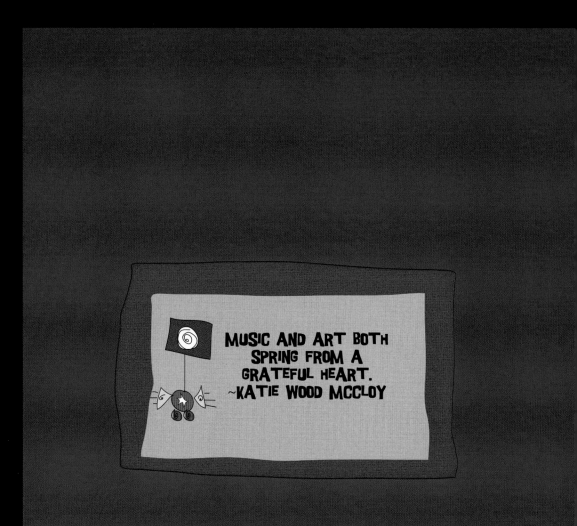

MUSIC AND ART BOTH
SPRING FROM A
GRATEFUL HEART.
~KATIE WOOD MCCLOY

NOVEMBER

1 B-day of **CARL SAGAN**, who said, "Somewhere, something incredible is waiting to be known." Step one: Close your eyes and just feel the essence of what that thought means without requiring yourself to do anything else about it. Step two: Imagine that the incredible thing waiting to be known is specifically for you. Step three: Trust that this is true.

2 B-day of writer **RAE WARDE**, who uses the phrase, "small and crappy" to lower her expectations to a place where she feels excited about starting her writing instead of immobilized by perfectionism. Try it: Choose something creative and start by striving for "small and crappy." Notice if it liberates you. If it doesn't, pretend like it does, and practice cooperating with yourself.

3 B-day of writer **DAWN KOTZER**, who offers these creative remedies: "Quick fix for a sore throat–freeze a table-spoon of honey . . . then suck slowly on the frozen honey and listen to the stories your throat tells you as it is soothed by this polar sweetness."

"Quick fix for a sore head . . . stop reading, lay still again and see if you can feel the stillest part of your interior body. 'Draw' a circle around it . . . and slip through it into oblivion."

Write a list of imaginatively clever remedies for anything from the sniffles to existential angst. Don't be afraid of being silly—it's a remedy for being too grown-up.

4 B-day of humorist **WILL ROGERS**, who said, "There are three kinds of men. The ones that learn by readin'. The few who learn by observation. The rest of them have to pee on the electric fence for themselves." Write a list of times you peed on the fence, so to speak, and found out the hard way. Congratulate yourself for the wisdom you gleaned. Choose a few of the stories, and translate them into poetry with short haiku or three -line poems of any number of syllables.

5 Write a poem or a short prose piece about yourself in **SECOND PERSON** perspective and if you like, beginning with this: "You are almost . . ."

6 B-day of novelist, **MICHAEL CUNNINGHAM**, who wrote "The secret of flight is this: you have to do it immediately, before your body realizes it is defying the laws."
Same with the creative process. Sometimes you have to jump in without hesitation, before your inner critic realizes what you're doing. Put the book down and go do something creative quickly. I'm not kidding.

7 B-day of **ALBERT CAMUS** who said, "Always go too far, because that's

where you'll find the truth." Write or create something and allow yourself to go too far, whether it's a journal entry, poetry, prose. . . explore "too far" and see what truths you discover. You may need to return to this creative act a few times to really penetrate your façade and discover the reward of moving past former stopping places.

8 B-day of singer-songwriter **BONNIE RAITT**, who said, "There's nothing like living a long time to create a depth and soulfulness in your music," and "I would rather feel things in extreme than not at all." Throughout your life, what were the things you felt in extreme? Choose one of them and speak about it on the page (poem, haiku, narration of a feeling deeply incident, expressive art). I seem to feel deeply about Broadway musicals as evidenced by bursting out in tears during songs and almost always tearing-up at the end when the cast return on stage. My haiku:

Broadway musicals
Move me in ways unspoken,
Smearing mascara.

9 B-day of poet **ANNE SEXTON**, who said,

> ### "POETRY IS MY LOVE,
> ### MY POSTMARK,
> ### MY HANDS, MY KITCHEN,
> ### MY FACE."

She was in and out of mental institutions all her life, and she said that poetry was the only thing that kept her alive. She said, "My fans think I got well, but I didn't: I just became a poet." What part of the creative process heals you? When's the last time you used it? How 'bout doing a word pool right now? Use some or all of these words, add more for poetry, prose, a diatribe or a prayer: rear view mirror, novel, begin, important, forget, sky scraper, partake, notice, hat, vermilion, forever, muster, gate, dandelion, stream, peculiar, vision, perpendicular, figure out, example, never mind, plate, principle, fortune

10 B-day of poet **JAMES BROUGHTON**, who said, "There is nothing more surprising than right now. Right now is where you always are anyway." Welcome to where you are anyway. Percolator question: What's happening right NOW?
Keep going with, or repeat the following sentence with different completions: "Right now . . ." Use details that you might not normally consider. Choose a different thinking cap to use with the word "now".

11 B-day of **KURT VONNEGUT**, who said, "I urge you to please notice when you are happy, and exclaim or murmur or think at some point, 'If this isn't nice, I don't know what is.'" Make a list of possible things you can do or think about related to that quote.

12 "THE ARTS ARE NOT A WAY TO MAKE A LIVING. THEY ARE A VERY HUMAN WAY OF MAKING LIFE MORE BEARABLE. YOU WILL GET AN ENORMOUS REWARD. YOU WILL HAVE CREATED SOMETHING."
~KURT VONNEGUT

Muse about how this quote applies to you. How do you make your life more bearable? And is there some creative endeavor that you can simply add for enjoyment?

13 The B-day of **ROBERT LOUIS STEVENSON**, who said, "I travel not to go anywhere, but to go. I travel for travel's sake. The great affair is to move." He is describing what it means to embrace the process. Can you engage in the creative process not with a destination in mind, but just for creativity's sake, and have an affair with the process? Suggestions: Photograph textures, write about spices.

14 Use a **SPATULA** for Loose-Association Practice:
List all associations you have to the word or the actual utensil. What else could a spatula be used for? Go for both the practical and the absurd. What memories, ideas, notions, acronyms. and silliness do you have related to a spatula. List at least twenty associations. Or keep going in the interest of forming new brain pathways which will gift you with more resourcefulness in any area of your life. Flip from procrastinator to doer. Flip a flop and make it a success with a new definition.

15 Artist **GEORGIA O'KEEFFE'S** B-day. When asked why she chose flowers as her subject, she said, "Because they're cheaper than models and they don't move." Choose one subject and do a body of work around it; for instance five to fifteen doodles, pieces of writing, or forms of art about apples, a spatula, a certain still life arrangement of high heels and marigolds, mailboxes, fairies, doorknobs, the number "9", your toaster, noses, the shape of whatever.

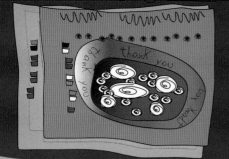

16 Line from the movie **DEAD POET'S SOCIETY**: "This is a battle, a war, and the casualties could be your hearts and souls." Don't let anyone tell you what you want. Decide for yourself, pursue your passion, do it in the name of your heart and soul.

17 B-day of **LORNE MICHAELS**, creator of Saturday Night Live who said, "People go to the zoo and they like the lion because it's scary. And the bear because it's intense, but the monkey makes people laugh." Jean Houston said, "At the height of laughter, the universe is flung into a kaleidoscope of new possibilities." Translated from French, Nicolas Chamfort said, "The most wasted of all days is that in which we have not laughed." Milton Berle said, "Laughter is an instant vacation." When's the last time you laughed? Making a record of what makes you laugh keeps things we tend to forget available for those days when reliving the levity can shift us into a better place: mirth. Reread something that made you laugh.

18 B-day of novelist **MARGARET ATWOOD**, who's last line of her novel, *The Handmaid's Tale*, reads "Are there any questions?" Write a piece, short or long, that also ends with that sentence.

19 B-day of screenwriter and director **CHARLIE KAUFMANN**, who in the movie, *Adaptation* wrote, "There are too many ideas and things and people. Too many directions to go. I was starting to believe the reason it matters to care passionately about something, is that it whittles the world down to a more manageable size."
Focusing on your creative passion, eliminating some of the distractions around you, is one way to make your world more manageable.
Choose an idea and make it your world. List or mind-map, "world" and write about or make art about a world.

It's a cruel and random world, but the chaos is all so beautiful.
~Hiromu Arakawa

20 Write a quick response to each of these: Your **CREATIVE PROCESS;** being: a color, a movement, a musical instrument, something in nature, something flying through the sky, a piece of clothing, a voice yelling sweet nothings at you, something you drop into the ocean to see what happens, something you ride, something you bake in the oven; or the wind.

21 B-day of English novelist **BERYL BAINBRIDGE**, who said, "The older one becomes, the quicker the present fades into sepia and the past looms up in glorious technicolour." Write a list of colors and then loosely associate, with no concern for logic, what memories might go with each of those colors. For example: Green is for rolling in the grass, which always seemed like a better idea than it actually was (cinch bugs). Blue is for the majesty of ocean in Miami and my dad's eyes.

22 B-day of author **ANDRE GIDE,** who said, "Be faithful to that which exists within yourself," and "Dare to be yourself."

But there are many selves inside we can choose from, depending on a given mood and circumstance. List the selves to whom you would like to stay faithful and describe three actions or thoughts that characterize each. Think of a time when it was easy to be yourself and think of some times in the future that might be like that too.

23 B-day of poet, **JENNIFER MICHAEL HECHT,** who wrote in *The Happiness Myth: The Historical Antidote to What Isn't Working Today*, "How was life before Pop-Tarts, Prozac and padded playgrounds? They ate strudel, took opium and played on the grass."
Write some observations using alliteration with the letter of your choice like Jennifer did with the letter "P."

EACH OF US MUST DO SOMETHING THAT MAKES OUR HEART SING, BECAUSE NOBODY WILL WANT TO DO IT WITH US IF WE ARE NOT PASSIONATE AND INSPIRED.
~DALAI LAMA

The world doesn't make sense, so why should I paint pictures that do?
~Pablo Picasso

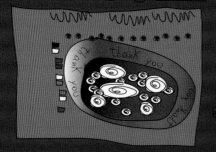

24 B-day of novelist **LAURENCE STERNE**. His big success was a novel called *The Life and Opinions of Tristram Shandy*, which was the first novel about writing a novel. Write about your approach to the process of creating—what's your technique? What works were your favorite, most difficult, most trans-formative? Embellish and write about yourself with eccentricities, dangerous habits, and strange obsessions about being swirly and esoteric.

25 B-day of physician and essayist, **LEWIS THOMAS**, who wrote, "We are, perhaps, uniquely among the earth's creatures, the worrying animal. We worry away our lives, fearing the future, discon-tent with the present, unable to take in the idea of dying, unable to sit still." And he also said, "The great secret of doctors, known only to their wives, but still hidden from the public, is that most things get better by themselves; most things, in fact, are better in the morning." Most every-thing we worry about never ends up happening. What are some worries you have and what are some thoughts you might want to replace them with? Write a short poem or haiku about things being better in the morning.

26 In the film, *Mona Lisa Smile*, Julia Roberts plays an art professor who says about van Gogh, "He painted what he felt, not what he saw. People didn't understand; to them it seemed childlike and crude. It took years for them to recognize his actual technique. To see the way his brushstrokes seemed to make the night sky move." Doodle, photograph, or paint several different renditions of the concept of movement. Be free like a child.

27 Make a list of at least ten ways you can pay homage to the words, "**THANK YOU.**" Choose a few and follow-through. Or go for a walk to the rhythm of saying thank you over and over as you think of your blessings.

28 B-day of **JON STEWART,** who said, "Insomnia is my greatest inspiration." Write an acronym for INSOMNIA. Here's mine: **I**nspiration **N**otifying **S**leepless **O**af: **M**ove **N**eurons **I**nto **A**ction.

29 B-day of writer **C.S. LEWIS,** who said, "You can make anything by writing." Choose one of these and "make": a compassionate declaration, a truce with yourself, a silly poem that doesn't make any sense, a journey to the cellar of your endearments, an attic of dreams stored in fancy boxes, or anything your creative intuition guides you to do.

30 B-day of **MARK TWAIN,** who said, "Twenty years from now you will be more disappointed by the things that you didn't do than by the ones you did do. So throw off the bowlines. Sail away from the safe harbor. Catch the trade winds in your sails. Explore. Dream. Discover." I've read that quote hundreds of times and will again, as many times as I need to keep remembering its truth. Remember to have a **REMINDER RITUAL** to remind yourself of quotes that fortify you and the things that work for you.

RULES ARE A
GREAT WAY TO
GET IDEAS.
ALL YOU HAVE
TO DO IS BREAK
THEM.
~JACK FOSTER

DECEMBER
MAINTENANCE

1 B-day of **WOODY ALLEN**, who said, "If you're not failing every now and again, it's a sign you're not doing anything very innovative." Review some things in your life that you consider failures, and reframe yourself as an innovator versus a failure. Write an acronym or acrostic for INNOVATE.

2 Take this **ANNE PACHETT** quote, sit with it, and see where it beckons you to go in thought, writing, art, or movement: "Writing is a job, a talent, but it's also the place to go in your head. It is the imaginary friend you drink your tea with in the afternoon."

3 B-day of writer, **JOSEPH CONRAD**, who said, "I begrudge each moment I spend away from paper. Inspiration comes to me while looking at the paper. Not writing, but just looking at the paper." Try just looking at the paper . . . and not writing or drawing. Have the paper tell you where it wants you to take it. Or if you're itching to do something, have the paper write about looking at *you*.

4 Find two or more **IMAGES** and connect them in writing or art. Or if you're in a place that's image-challenged, borrow these images: a bridge, an unmailed letter, and a woman standing three feet off the ground - write, sketch, doodle . . . daydream.

5 B-day of writer **CALVIN TRILLIN**. Write about a recent meal you had as if you were a food editor even if the meal was just the usual grilled cheese and tomato soup. Give the meal a flowery culinary title and description or a cranky critic response. Have fun with it. Play with various Thinking Caps: serious, another absurd, detail-oriented, free-spirited, edgy, confused, an alien, a little kid, a street person, the Queen of Hearts.

6 PAINT SAMPLE NAMES just cry out for creative connection. Take the names below and let them trigger writing ideas, or take each color and list memories of things or events that those colors evoke. Rename the colors:

Kinda Coffee	Sage Before Beauty	Slightly Angry	Not Blue
Shell White	Navy Wannabe	Lost in Moss	Blue Sky
Somewhere	Somewhere Else	Melted Hershey	Dishwater
Alabastard	The New Black	Not That Mad	Motherboard
Beige Watch	Inner Eyelid	Nasturtium	Sheer Green

Sheer Green reminds me of the color of a business suit I wore when I was in the corporate world. Sheer glad I don't wear suits anymore.
Shell White reminds me of finding shells on Florida beaches; Shell if I know where I put them .
Melted Hershey reminds me that there's a not-melted one in the fridge, gotta go.

7 B-day of **TOM WAITS**, who, once when he got a melody in his head when he was driving, asked his Muse, "Excuse me, can't you see that I'm driving?" Write a letter to your Muse requesting collaboration on the logistics of reporting ideas and inspiration. Optional: Have your Muse answer.

8 HIDE, (the holidays can be a good time for that) or mind-map the word "hide" and surround it with associations, images, characters, and stories that come to mind, then leave it at that or see what it inspires you to want to do. Or write an acronym or acrostic for the word HIDE. If you're not in a hiding mood, just run around the living room, the backyard, or in the food court of a shopping mall not hiding a thing. Be careful not to knock the ornaments off the tree.

9 Go outside, **LET THE AIR TOUCH YOU**, and remind you that you're alive. Close your eyes and invite an idea to awaken some passion in you. If that doesn't work, act as if it does. If that doesn't work, open the dictionary to the last two numbers of your birth year, pick a word, and let it trigger writing or doodling.

10 B-day of poet **EMILY DICKINSON**. Reading someone's well-crafted words can be inspiration in and of itself for art or further writing. Keep going with the following Emily quote or make it into art, collage, or a dance.

"To live is so startling it leaves little time for anything else."

TO LIVE IS SO STARTLING IT LEAVES LITTLE TIME FOR ANYTHING ELSE

11 Birthday of writer **JIM HARRISON,** who wrote 10 books between the ages of sixty and seventy alone. He said: "After a few years of possible overproductivity, I had to take a break 'cause I was getting goofy. I was even making up paragraphs when I walked to the mailbox. I couldn't go anyplace without writing it." Wouldn't that be nice? Let Jim Harrison's story break a few of your limiting beliefs today. Extra credit: get goofy.

12 Write down 3 or 4 **THOUGHTS** you think that are not serving your creativity. Then take a moment to review each thought and ask yourself how you would feel and what you would do if you didn't have those thoughts.

13 Your **HANDS** are filled with stories, dance, movement, and possibility. Make a list of all the creative possibilities associated with hands. Consider their familiar look, scars, and individuality.

14 B-day of writer, **SHIRLEY JACKSON**, who wrote, "Am I walking toward something I should be running away from?" Has this question ever applied anywhere in your life? Relay how it has or invent how it might. If you're short on time, write a list of ways it applies, or write short three line poems. Abbreviated forms of creative expression are skill building so don't discount doing something quickly and small versus nothing at all.

15 Keep going with your own writing with one or more of these **STARTERS:**
After years of . . .
The only way I'm going . . .
There are forty-five . . .

16 B-day of singer/songwriter **JILL BRYAN**, who said, "When we choose to let go of our perpetual busyness, even for a few short moments, we give ourselves an amazing gift . . . a tranquil time and space to allow new creative thoughts to form and effortlessly bubble to the surface of our mind."
Close your eyes, put some music on, and let go of the busyness. Write an acronym or acrostic for TRANQUIL.

17 Lie on the floor and let all the tension of your life melt, sink, and soften. Creativity needs **RELAXATION.** I enjoy lying under the Christmas Tree.

18 Rainer Maria Rilke said, "But your **SOLITUDE** will be a support and a home for you, even in the midst of very unfamiliar circumstances, and from it you will find all your paths." Find some solitude today . . . away from social media, the Internet, and the TV and notice what happens. Write an acrostic for "solitude."

19 Stare at something **FAMILIAR** until it becomes something unfamiliar. Write about it for 3 minutes. Repeat. If it doesn't work, let it go and Google "unfamiiar."

20 B-day of poet W. B. Yeats' lifelong muse, **MAUD GONNE**. To one of Yeats' marriage proposals she replied, "You would not be happy with me. You make beautiful poetry out of what you call your unhappiness and you are happy in that. Marriage would be such a dull affair. Poets should never marry." Don't get divorced (unless you want to), but write poetry about an unhappiness—it's one of the silver linings.

21 Today is the **WINTER SOLSTICE**, the shortest day and longest night in the Northern Hemisphere. Write a haiku, poem, or prose piece from or to the night. Make a visual journaling page, doodle, or painting. Or place the title, "What the Night Said," at the top of the page and let the energy of the solstice power your writing or art. Also the birthday of **FRANK ZAPPA**. He was a self-taught composer and performer, and his diverse musical influences led him to create music that was often impossible to categorize. Food for thought on long nights.

22 Take a notebook to 3 places today and list all of the **SOUNDS YOU HEAR.** Notice how present this makes you. The more present you are the more you open your creative conduits.

23 B-day of poet **ROBERT BLY**, who said , "A lazy part of us is like a tumbleweed. It doesn't move on its own. Sometimes it takes a lot of Depression to get tumbleweeds moving." Make a list of things that have gotten you moving in the past.

24 Write a **LIST OF MEMORIES,** any order. Just write whatever comes to mind, insignificant AND significant—write them all.

25 CHRISTMAS Yule be Okay. If you have a hard time with the holidays, invent imaginary friends, bodyguards, and other creative entitiess. Inventing new coping skills is a great creative exercise, accepting yourself for however you feel may be a new point of view that warrants exploration. If you are a Christmas Elf . . . celebrate.

26 B-day of writer **HENRY MILLER,** who said, "Everyone has his own reality in which, if one is not too cautious, timid, or frightened, one swims. This is the only reality there is." What three messages do you want to repeatedly give yourself in the coming year which will create your reality? Example: "I can't wait to see what I come up with today."

27 Have an **AWARDS CEREMONY** for the past year: Write down winners for best man, woman, moment, vacation, movie, book, learning experience, accomplishment, funny moment of the year. Choose them from people you admired in your personal life or someone who made news.

28 B-day of *Saturday Night Live* head-writer **SETH MEYERS**, who shared that *SNL* writers have different ways of coming up with material for jokes. He himself prefers to listen to the NPR morning news while playing soccer video games on his Xbox. Doing two things at once actually helps many creative people relax enough to allow ideas to come through. Try a combination of activities to ignite some writing or art ideas today. If you need a starter, use one of these unfinished sentences: "I feel as if …", or "I forgot about the ocean…"

29 Go back through the manual and do a prompt you missed. Or just relax creatively.

30 B-day of **RUDYARD KIPLING**. Reflect in visual journaling or journal writing on this quote and what means to you:"Of all the liars in the world, sometimes the worst are our own fears."

31 NEW YEARS EVE and B-day of painter **HENRI MATISSE**. His paintings expressed emotion with wild, often dissonant colors, without regard for the subject's natural colors. He broke the painting rules of his time. Write a set of new rules for how you will show up in the coming year just for the exercise of being a wild inventor. Let this simply be an exercise in creative thought without pressure to actually follow the rules. Make the rules a poem, a rhythmic list, a rap, a pronounce-ment. Invent absurd rules, as well as radically kind and thoughtful ones. Defy the limitations of rules. Do a collage of your new rules . . . just for fun.

HAVE A HOLIDAY PARADE IN YOUR HEAD. WAVE* GOOD-BYE TO THE OLD YEAR AND WELCOME IN THE NEW.

*Like a parade queen.

BELIEVE

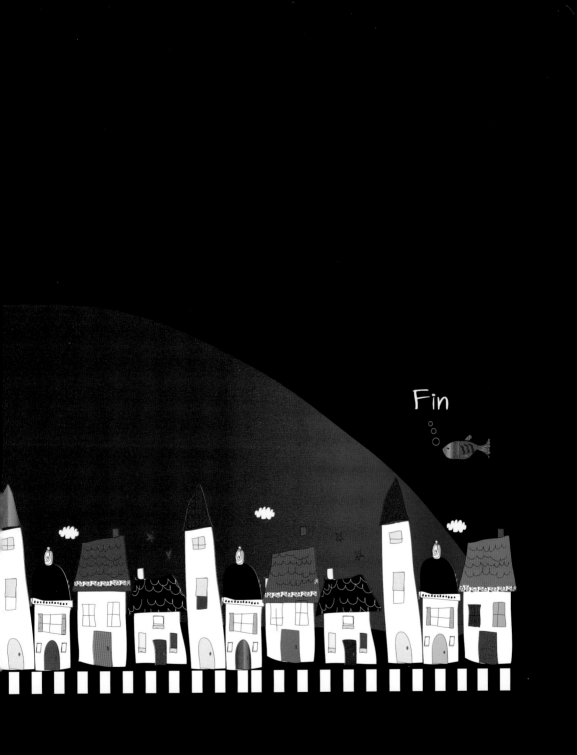

Fin

Thank you to All My Readers.

(That would be you.)

ALSO TO:

Jennifer Kasius for believing in this project,
Stephanie Kip-Rostan—my stellar agent, Monica Parcell,
Bill Jones, Seta Zink, and all the other peeps at Running Press.

Special heartfelt thanks to my spiritual teacher,
Jacob Glass.

Also to Rae Warde, Dawn Kotzer, Janet Whitehead,
Jennifer Farr-Jones, Lisa Jaffee, Reba Spencer, Kat Kirby,
Chris Dunmire, Pam Ellis, Jill Allison Bryan, Steve Fix, Apara Kohl,
all my fun friends on Facebook who keep me belly-laughing and inspired,
(I don't have room for all of you, it would take up ten more pages and
I'm already two pages over, so fill your name in here _____)
Marney Madridakis, Bert Lawrence, Meredith Deal, Zoya Zolinikoff, Don
Soloman, Harvey Huff, Rick Christensen, Donna Gray, Kris Powell,
Alice Bandy, Jim Billingsley, Alex & Traci Bosworth, Bobby McFerrin,
Sparkle Wood, Denis Leary, Kim Cromwell, Bethany Crandell, Liz Fulcher,
Pattie Mosca, Gary Johnston, Tom Waits, Ellen DeGeneres, Tim Badonsky,
all the KMCC coaches and Muse Facilitators whom enrich my life,
all my teachers, guides, and students,
my cats: Mambo and Sappho.
And I couldn't have done it without being here: thanks Mom and Dad.

To keep your creativity running smoothly, there will be conspiracies to play
with the inner-workings of **The Owner's Manual** among kindred and
quirky spirits, so don't miss the fun, subscribe to the Muse Letter at
www.themuseisin.com and visit The Awe-manac Page on Facebook.

Peace, love, and fireflies,

Jill Badonsky

Jill Badonsky, M.Ed. is founder and director of Kaizen-Muse Creativity Coaching and has been spreading the joy of creativity since 1980.

She is author of *The Awe-manac, A Daily Dose of Wonder* and *The Nine Modern Day Muses, (and a Bodyguard): 10 Guides to Creative Inspiration.*

Jill is also a multi-media artist, poet, corporate drop-out, workshop leader, creative consultant, yoga teacher and key-note speaker. She wrote and starred in the one-woman show, *I Can't Always Handle Reality But It's Really the Only Place to Get a Good Cup of Coffee*, but currently has cut back on both reality and coffee.

Jill lives in a treehouse, herds cats, and engages in spontaneous interpretive dances.

Visit her at www.themuseisin.com, www.kaizenmuse.com, on Facebook and Twitter.

THOUGH NO ONE CAN GO BACK AND MAKE A BRAND-NEW START, ANYONE CAN START FROM NOW AND MAKE A BRAND-NEW ENDING.
-CARL BARD